John Redwood, Member of Parliament for Wokingham and a prolific commentator on constitutional and economic issues, served as Secretary of State for Wales between 1993 and 1995. His previous books include *Popular Capitalism*, *The Global Marketplace*, *The Death of Britain?* and, most recently, *Stars and Strife: The Coming Conflicts Between the USA and the European Union*.

Just Say No!

100 arguments
against the euro

John Redwood

Politico's
PUBLISHING

First published in Great Britain 2001
Politico's Publishing
8 Artillery Row
Westminster
London
SW1P 1RZ

www.politicospublishing.co.uk

A catalogue record for this book is available from the British Library.

ISBN 1 902301 99 4

Printed and bound by Bell and Bain, Scotland

Contents

Europe is my continent, not my country

Europe is my continent, not my country. It includes Switzerland and Norway, Poland and Hungary, the eastern European countries as well as France, Germany and the other members of the European Union. I want to help build a Europe that is more prosperous, that is democratic, that respects the different languages, cultures, religions and histories of the European peoples. We can do that by extending the common market eastwards, by encouraging more co-operation and agreement between governments, and by supporting democratic institutions in each and every country. A single currency will damage democracy and get in the way of prosperity. The British people do not want to join the euro. They are right to be sceptical. They should just say 'No'.

Advocates of a single currency for twelve countries in western Europe make two main claims for it: prosperity and peace. To them, it makes business and economic sense. They think it would save business the costs and uncertainties of exchange-rate movements. They look forward to a single currency world of lower interest rates and faster growth. However, the single currency will mean high unemployment and slow growth in some parts of the union, and inflation in others. There is no single interest rate that is right for Ireland and Sicily, east Germany and southern England.

For most British businesses it would be all cost and no benefit. They would have to change all their tills, slot and cash machines, but they have no DM or French franc revenue to exchange.

Many supporters of the scheme see it as a much more fundamental issue than one of slower or faster growth. They see it as a matter of peace or war. They think that the single currency would be a major step on the road to a united Europe, where the disagreements and tensions between races, peoples, governments and religions would be a thing of the past. They want to abolish the risk of war between countries in western Europe by turning the countries that have been to war with each other into regions in the new Europe.

They look to the United States as an example of how it could work. They overlook how unfortunate this analogy is. The USA was born of a war to throw off British rule, extended by a war against Mexico in the push south and west, and finally united at the point of many a rifle in a murderous civil war between the states of the union. The USA only became one, the south was only won, when the uprising of the reluctant states was quelled by superior forces. I do not want a Europe like that, and see no reason to follow the USA's example.

The single-currency scheme has already generated tension. There have been riots on the streets of France against the spending cuts the currency scheme requires. Three-quarters of the German people are opposed to the abolition of the DM despite their government's insistence that it must go ahead. One in twelve Germans, one in ten French people, one in nine Italians and almost one in seven Spaniards are out of work. Despite that, their governments think that donning the single currency hair shirt is more important than promoting growth and prosperity.

I want Britain to explain the damage this idea is now doing. We must remind Europe that the peace has been kept since 1945 by NATO, not by the European Union. We should explain that a peace-loving, democratic Germany is very different from the Germany of Hitler. We should remind people that the balance of power has shifted decisively with the rise of the USA as the world's only super-power. We should explain that we now live in a global market and a global world of fast communications. The idea of integrating between six and fifteen western European countries is old-fashioned and backward-looking. The danger is that Europe will become a high-tax backwater, cut off from the dynamic trade and investment opportunities of Asia, and isolated from the technical advances coming from both east and west.

You cannot have a single currency without a single interest rate, a single banking policy, a single budget and a single finance minister or central bank governor. You are led inevitably to a single taxation policy and a single economic policy. You are close to creating a single government.

Recent trends in Europe have been to create more countries and currencies, not fewer. If anything, the peoples of Europe want to live in smaller countries, not bigger ones. We have seen all the former Comecon countries replace the rouble with their own national money: they saw no advantage in a single common currency. No one can say the rouble made them rich. We have seen the Irish split away from the pound and set up their own punt. Growth accelerated after they did so. We have seen Yugoslavia fracture into many pieces.

A Europe of nations is the only Europe that can work. It must be a Europe of nations protected from threat by NATO, friendly with the USA and Asia, open to the world, not closed to parts of it. Europe's problem is not that it has too many currencies, but that it has too few jobs. It does not need to reduce the variety of money, but it does need to cut the amount of regulation and legislation.

The euro: a sickly baby

Abolishing the pound would be bad for our wealth and our democracy. It would mean higher taxes. Once in a currency union with France and Germany, British taxpayers would have to accept some responsibility for the less well off parts of the union. Extra tax would have to be levied in the UK to send more subsidies to east Germany and northern France. If a currency area is too big, it means that the interest rates suit no particular part of it. In many places, interest rates would be higher than they should be, cutting back on investment, limiting spending power, overpricing mortgages and destroying jobs.

The single currency is no mere technical event for discussion by bankers alone. It implies a single economic policy for all the parts of the currency union. It would lead to more and more control over our budget being assumed by the European authorities. The Maastricht treaty, which created the new currency, sets out how the European authorities would control the amount our country could borrow. Now, naturally, the European Union is seeking more authority over how our government taxes and how it spends.

One of the main themes of this book is that changing currencies is an important part of changing countries. Many Europeans, like me, are not ready to change countries. We owe our loyalty to our nation, not to the new union. I do not believe it is going to be possible to govern a single country called Europe from Brussels and Frankfurt, given the different languages, histories, cultures, identities and attitudes of the different peoples of the member states of the union.

One of the paradoxes of the move towards European union is the attitude towards a Europe of the regions. The advancing centralisation of federal power claims to be making some of its advances in the name of greater regional autonomy. It allies itself with Catalan nationalism, Basque separatism, Scottish nationalism and with those who would like northern and southern Italy to split. It does so with no apparent sense of irony, yet there is a fundamental irony in those who are seeking to extend central control doing so in the name of greater local autonomy. Those in the separatist and nationalist movements of regional Europe will discover one day, if they persevere with their unholy alliance, that they have substituted for national authority a far worse international authority. Brussels may become more powerful and more remote than the authority they have thrown off. A single currency is not delivering more economic policy power to the regions. It is taking more away from the regions and giving it to the unelected European Central Bank in Frankfurt.

This book looks at the economic arguments and sets out how the scheme might easily miscarry. It begins by showing what went wrong with the Exchange-Rate Mechanism which, was a practice run for the single currency. When the ERM collapsed, the architects of the euro should have seen it as a warning to Europe that the states are not ready for a single economy and currency. If countries cannot keep their exchange rates in line with each other, they have not come together sufficiently to consider sharing a currency.

Far from helping the City of London to grow and dominate, its inclusion in a euro zone might be deeply damaging to the flexible global marketplace in the City. Far from helping the European economy to recover, the scheme for currency union began by extending the recession and made economic growth rather more difficult. It was only when the value of the euro plunged that European industry was able to recover a little.

I also examine the costs and pain of transition. For most British businesses, the single currency is all cost and no benefit. Most serve only a local or national market: there will be no savings on foreign-exchange transaction costs for them, should Britain join the single currency. Conversely, like all businesses, they will have to double their number of tills when collecting cash from the public, change over all their slot machines and cash-handling machinery and change their accounting systems to accommodate the new currency. For up to six months in a transition period, shops will have to be able to collect both the euro and sterling: they will need much greater working balances and working capital. If the pound is finally removed from price tickets, it will be like shopping with a foreign currency. People's sense of values will be disrupted, as they mentally try to convert euros into pounds, multiplying by somewhere between 1.2 and 1.4.

It is time for Britain to wake up to the magnitude of the changes being proposed. You cannot have a single currency without a single budget and a single government to enforce it. You certainly cannot have a single-currency union where the economies are as different in their performance as the economies of western Europe. You cannot have a successful single country where people speak eleven different languages and have such different attitudes. You cannot have a flourishing democracy if all the important decisions about interest rates, credit, borrowing and the government deficit are taken out of the hands of the democratic process and given to a group of unelected officials.

On 1 January 1999, the euro was launched to great acclaim, both in Europe and in the British media. We were told that the euro would be a strong currency. There would be such demand for it that its value would soar. No one could be without it in their portfolio. It was time to fill your boots.

We were told that the euro would soon rival the mighty dollar. It would not just be strong, it would be formidable, the world's most powerful and desirable money.

We were told that it was an historic accomplishment on the road to European union. It would bring about the harmonious integration that has always been the euro advocates' holy grail.

The reality was different. For most of its first two years, the new currency struggled in the markets. Month after month, its value plummeted. Beginning at $1.17, it fell below $1 and then below 90 cents. Against the pound, it fared little better. It began life worth 71 pence and fell to 58 pence at its worst point so far. Many investors who bought the story of euro invincibility at the outset reversed their position as the slide got underway. They were soon caught up in the general pessimism. The German public sceptical at best, became more hostile the further the euro fell. They had been promised a strong currency to replace the mighty Deutschmark, only to discover they were lumbered with the opposite. It was only as 2000 drew to its close that some investors began to feel the dollar had done too well for too long, and some balance returned to the market for the euro. If the euro climbs back towards its opening level, there will be rejoicings in the pro-euro camp, but their claims will be treated with more scepticism because their initial predictions were so wrong.

The euro has not become a serious rival to the US dollar. The main transactions in international currency markets are dominated by the dollar, which accounts for the largest share of international trade. The euro is throwing up predictable squabbles and tensions within the EU. The UK, Denmark and Sweden, which remain outside the euro group, are debarred from the main meetings on economic strategy for the euro area. Ireland, with a fast-moving economy more in tune with the Anglo-Saxon bloc than with Euroland, has had to experience interest rates that are far too low for her, leading to an unwelcome acceleration of inflation. Greece has struggled to catch up, but will now be allowed to join following a devaluation and a period in the modern version of the ERM at the new rate.

For Britain, entry into the euro would be very bad news. There are ten overriding reasons why we should say 'No':

Ten reasons to say 'No'

1   The costs of conversion are huge. Every slot machine, accounting system, computer, vending machine and bank telling machine would need to be replaced or altered. Many shops would need two sets of tills for the long six-month conversion period when both currencies are legal tender. For most businesses, it is all cost and no benefit.

2   People will find it difficult to acquire a sense of value in the new currency. When one euro is worth somewhere between 58p and 71p (the range so far), converting is not easy. During the six-month transition, you will need lots of different change for the car park and other ticket machines. You will need two lots of coins in different currencies. It will be like going shopping in a foreign country – all fumbles and no sense of value.

3   The nation's gold and currency reserves will be passed over to the European Central Bank. They will no longer be ours to do with as we wish. It's like being asked to hand over your deposit account to the local council for their use. Joining a single currency is like taking out a joint bank account with the neighbours. How can we be sure we will get a fair share?

4   We will always have the wrong interest rates. We found when we were in the ERM and shadowing the DM that rates were either too low, so we had inflation, or too high, so many firms went bankrupt and house prices fell. One interest rate cannot fit all.

5   Under the rules of the single currency, we would lose control of the national budget. We would have to accept European controls on how much the UK can borrow. That means we would have to either put taxes up or cut spending during a downturn, when public borrowing usually rises. Joining the euro means accepting the rules of the bank manager in Frankfurt.

6 Single-currency areas always include regional policies, to send money from the rich parts of the union to the poorer parts. We do this in the UK, the sterling currency union. The EU will need bigger transfers of cash from richer regions, such as most of the UK, to the poorer parts such as east Germany and southern Italy. Inside the euro, we will have to pay more tax to send money to east Germany and Sicily.

7 The City of London is one of the world's big three financial markets, and provides many jobs in the UK. It is flourishing offshore from the euro zone. If we join the euro, London's financial institutions and banks will come under more EU regulation, which will drive some of the business offshore from us and from Euroland. Joining the euro will force business out of London to New York, Switzerland and Bermuda.

8 A single currency requires a single economic policy. The Euroland ministers and officials are already working on such a common economic policy. Given how badly the UK has done out of the common fisheries policy and the common agricultural policy, we should think twice before signing up to a common economic policy. Do we want the people who gave us the common agricultural policy and the common fisheries policy also controlling us through a common economic policy?

9 The main Euroland countries and the European Commission believe that a single market and single currency area also needs common taxation. They are busily trying to make VAT the first

EU-collected tax, trying to harmonise business taxes, and inventing new European taxes such as the art levy and the climate change levy. Euroland taxes are higher than the UK's. Joining the euro will mean higher taxes in Britain.

10 Sovereign countries always have their own currency. They do so because the decisions about how much money to put into circulation, how much to charge to borrow money, how much money the government can borrow and what to do with the nation's reserves or savings are all important and central to being sovereign. Join the euro and what is the point of general elections when so many of the important decisions about our prosperity will be taken behind closed doors by unelected officials in a far-away bank?

Chapter one

Creating a country called Europe

The idea of monetary union is an important element of a far bigger whole. It is part of a plan to create a new country called Europe that will be war-free and frontier-free. It reveals the misunderstanding behind Britain's membership of the European Community. When we joined the EEC in 1972, Britain was assured by leading politicians that this was a trade arrangement. It was called the Common Market. The then government made it clear in a white paper that Britain's sovereignty would not be damaged, that our legal system would remain the same and we would still be a parliamentary democracy.

All this was reinforced at the time of the referendum on British membership in 1975. We were told again that this was a trade arrangement; that it was essential for British jobs and prosperity, and that our main national interests and institutions would not be affected.

By 1992, the story had changed. A government paper issued to set out the Maastricht treaty, explaining the single currency to a British audience, dealt explicitly with the question of those who felt cheated. It tried to answer those who felt that the common market they had joined was metamorphosing into a European state without their consent. The paper stated: "The original Community treaties aimed at an ever closer union amongst the peoples of Europe." That is quite true, but that aspect of the Treaty of Rome did not hold centre stage in the case presented for joining, or the case presented to encourage us to vote "Yes" in the referendum campaign. The EEC was sold to the British people as a necessary way of protecting and extending their trade with the countries of western Europe. Indeed, it was implied that we would lose trade or be blocked in some way from trading so freely with the rest of Europe if we did not join.

As the 1992 white paper explained, Maastricht added new areas of European Community authority to an already substantial range. Some parts of education and health policy, vocational training, cultural policy, consumer protection, aid to developing countries, the development of trans-European networks and policies for industrial competitiveness were all added to a list that already encompassed agriculture, industry, trade, transport, budgetary policy, regional policy and much else besides.

The British government, conscious that the growing range of Community powers and actions was beginning to add up to an alternative government, stated clearly in 1992:

The Maastricht treaty itself requires that the national identities of member states shall be respected. Fundamental areas of national life, such as the monarchy, the relationship between Church and state, and the parliamentary system, cannot be touched by the Community. Getting the right balance between Community and national action is known as subsidiarity. It is now (for the first time) enshrined in the Maastricht treaty . . . The inclusion of this idea in the treaty marks a major change of direction in the Community.

The government clearly hoped that this would be true. However, the other members of the EEC and the European institutions saw Maastricht primarily as a treaty to push forward European union, rather than to reverse some of the powers already granted to European institutions by the Treaty of Rome and the Single European Act. The Treaty of Rome had expressed the aspiration of ever closer union. The Single European Act had introduced more qualified majority voting to erode the vetoes of member states over new policies, and now the Maastricht Treaty set out an overarching scheme of economic and monetary union. This was the ultimate end of the long economic journey begun in the 1950s with the Coal and Steel Community which brought together France and Germany through a common institution for their principal heavy industries. In 1998, the Treaty of Amsterdam added a common foreign policy with a single High Representative to express this policy to the world. In 2000, the Treaty of Nice removed many further vetoes over areas such as transport, trade, economic policy, regional policy and border controls, pressing the EU towards its destiny as a new country with a strong central government in Brussels. The idea of subsidiarity had not succeeded in changing the direction of the EU. If anything, the rush to full political, economic and monetary union became more rapid after Maastricht than before.

Successful states enjoy the loyalty and support of their citizens. People living within their boundaries accept the legitimacy of the state. They accept its main institutions, and they feel they belong to it. In western Europe, a sense of nationhood has developed at different times in different regions, and is felt with varying degrees of intensity in different countries. In some important cases, it is deep-rooted and goes back many centuries.

England has enjoyed a sense of nationhood and has accepted common governing institutions for more than a thousand years. France, too, developed early, with a national pride and common institutions of government in Paris. The UK emerged in the sixteenth and seventeenth centuries from the merger of England with Wales and then with Scotland, culminating in the Act of Union in 1707. Holland fought for her independence in the sixteenth century and flourished as a state from the seventeenth century. Denmark, Norway and Sweden broke their united Scandinavian kingdom, deciding that they were separate nations. Spain came together in fighting off the Moors during the fifteenth century. Italy and Germany were products of nine-teenth-century unification.

Minorities within some of these nations would like there to be two or more countries where currently one exists: some Catalans and Basques would like independence from Spain; north and south Italy have never been entirely reconciled to each other's company; Irish Nationalists in Ulster would like Northern Ireland to become part of the Republic of Ireland. Although these are important matters to those battling over them, they are details when compared with the larger picture, which shows us millions of people all over western Europe who feel strong loyalty to their own nation and who are broadly happy with the pattern of national government, national languages and national institutions they have inherited. In no case do people want fewer countries. In some cases, people want more countries, or wish to transfer to a different country.

There have been several attempts at a wider pan-European unity. The most recent was the attempt of the Soviet Union to unite the eastern and central European countries in a common empire. They enjoyed a common market, a common means of settlement, a common defence and foreign policy. They were allowed to keep their national governments, but these governments were very circumscribed in what they could do because their economies were controlled by Moscow through a single currency, the rouble, and a common economic and trade policy. Their foreign policies were dictated by Russian influence and a common army. They were prevented from having free elections in the western style. This experiment lasted for more than forty years, but it could be kept going only by the use of force. Few wanted to leave western Europe to settle in the new united east, although they were free to do so. Many wanted to leave the east and settle in the west. They were shot if they were detected when trying to do so.

While it is true that the main defect of this attempt at union was the Communist system that was being imposed, it is also true that revolts against it were national, not pan-national, popular uprisings. The collapse of Communism centred upon a series of separate revolutions in different countries. The first cries of the rebels were not anti-Communist, but demands to restore their flag, culture, currency and identity. In some countries, the Communist Party reformed, still espousing the old policy of central planning, and continued to attract a substantial number of votes. No party formed to oppose the resumption of national identity: everyone seemed to want that.

Even the very small states that had joined the union, such as Estonia, Latvia and Lithuania, all wished to emerge with their own independence. It proved that national loyalties are deep-rooted, and cannot be suppressed even after forty years of indoctrination. Forty years of Russians settling in these countries failed to make them vote to stay in the union. Many of the people who helped revolutions in those countries could not remember a time when their country had had its own currency and its own army, yet they knew that was what they wanted. In the one country where national identity did not immediately re-emerge, its peoples sought more states than had existed even before the Communist take-over: the peoples of Yugoslavia rejected Yugoslavia as another artificial union, preferring Bosnia, Croatia and Serbia, or even smaller regions, where they felt a sense of linguistic, religious and national identity.

The nearest Europe has come to a voluntary union of more states was in the later Middle Ages with the Holy Roman Empire. Then there were common languages for the educated: Latin for works of scholarship, and court French for diplomacy and conversation. There was a common currency in the form of gold, used in trade by the intrinsic value of the metal, whatever local or national symbols and suggestions of value might be stamped on it. There were some common governing institutions for the Low Countries and much of central Europe. The territory was much expanded in the sixteenth century, when Spain shared its monarch with the Holy Roman Empire. There was a common

17

enemy, the hordes of Islam to the south, and a common belief in Catholic Christianity.

All this was shattered by the fears of France and by a series of nationalist revolts, often connected with the emergence of Protestantism. In England and Wales, the change to Protestantism was precipitated by the government to strengthen England's independence as a nation. The main intent was to throw off the power of the papal courts and allow the King in Parliament to settle his own marriage and succession. Henry VIII was the first English Eurosceptic. In the Netherlands, Protestantism was tied up with resentment at Spanish rule, while several German states mixed their enthusiasm for throwing off the power of Rome with some scepticism about the value of imperial government.

European empires have usually been created and maintained by force. The Roman empire was established by force. Legions gradually conquered more and more of western Europe. The structure crumbled when the legions lost their grip. Napoleon's dream was to unite Europe under French military direction. For a few years, he was partially successful. Hitler tried to unite Europe under German military occupation, then attempted to purge it of the ethnic groups he did not want in his Aryan empire. The Austro-Hungarian empire fell to pieces when the imperial will declined. In each case, a European empire was replaced by smaller countries. It required force to hold the greater unity together. Cultural, linguistic and local identity are more powerful and longer lasting than any empire.

It is true that even a sense of identity will pass if it is not strong, or if something more powerful and appealing is offered, but this is rare. In my part of the UK, the home counties, people are happy to be both British and English. There is no yearning for Wessex, which was once a strong kingdom. Yet in Wales, which became part of a British governing system five hundred years ago, there is still a strong sense of Welsh identity. Even though four out of five Welsh residents cannot speak Welsh, and even though a strong majority want to remain part of the UK, Welsh identity is still most important. Language is often the crucial issue, but ethnic or religious differences matter too. People do not feel strongly about Wessex, because Wessex is loyal to the English language and the same Christian religion as England. Wales is loyal to its own language. Bosnia feels different from Serbia because of its ethnic and religious differences.

Both Hitler and Napoleon sought a united Continental Europe by war, diplomacy and alliances. Of course, there is no comparison between some of their methods, and the peaceful means to union of the present European project, and their vision of European union was unacceptable to many people in western Europe. They were unable to persuade people by diplomacy that theirs was the right approach. Again, it was nationalism of a more local kind that upset Napoleon's grand plans. In forming coalitions against him, Britain was able to appeal to people's fear of being dictated to by France against their own local and national interest.

In 1944–5, Britain and the USA were seen as liberators by most French people, even though France had a government that collaborated with the Germans, and by many in Italy, even though her government was a strong ally of Germany and shared Germany's war aims. Fascism was no more able to appeal to pan-nationalism than was Communism. These two evil tyrannies of the twentieth century were put down not just by force of arms, but by a sense of independence, freedom and national identity amongst the old nations of Europe.

Although things can and do change, and life moves on, we are all prisoners of history. It is most important to remind ourselves of history when trying to answer the question: could a new European state work? My answer is: It cannot.

History shows that union should be attempted only by consent, and should be achieved very slowly, if at all. It must demonstrate major benefits over the present arrangements. It must reassure people that their identity and interests are not threatened by it. It has never worked in the past based on force. It cannot work this time if it is based on withholding the truth from people. Abolish the pound and you abolish an important part of Britain: you make a decisive move towards a country called Europe governed from Brussels and Frankfurt.

One of the most worrying features of the argument in Britain has been the insistence by those who want more European integration that it has nothing to do with the creation of a single country or government. Yet reading the treaties and looking at the wide array of institutions already established in the name of the EU shows that the intention is the establishment of a new country. The union is keen to offer citizenship, and sees citizenship as a series of rights. A citizen of France or a subject of the

Queen in the UK has rights, but also responsibilities. I know that the British government will come to my aid abroad if I need it. I know that a British passport entitles me to enter most countries, and provides me with British embassy and consular support. I know that all British subjects have the right to a fair trial, to vote if they qualify on the electoral roll, and access to a wide range of public services. On the other hand, many of us are duty-bound to serve on juries, to be available, should a national emergency arise, to serve in the armed forces, to pay taxes and keep the Queen's peace.

The new European concept of citizenship was clearly designed by public-relations minds: it appears to be all rights and no duties, but on closer examination it comprises both. The European citizen now has the right to vote in European parliamentary elections and in local elections wherever he or she may be resident in the union, to travel throughout the union showing only an identity card, to use the embassy and consular arrangements which the union is now establishing direct or through member states, and to take a case to the European court. Under the provisions of the Treaty of Nice, the union is working towards common frontiers, a common visa system, a common policy on asylum and legal settlement, and a common method of border enforcement.

The responsibilities are indirect. Each citizen is required to pay taxes, but to their national authorities, who are then obliged to send them to the union authorities. Union armies are still in an embryo stage. There are some joint actions between the armies of member states, and now the formation of a euro corp. Enlisting the troops is still the responsibility of each member state, but in more and more cases the armies are there to back up a common European foreign policy settled at union level.

From time to time, the union buttresses its position with the citizenry by urging a "people's Europe". Ideas have included easier travel, easier trade, more cultural and educational exchanges, more language learning, and the single currency to facilitate shopping in different member states.

The concentration on presentation has led to the development of the flag and logo. The twelve-stars symbol, yellow on a blue background, has become the EU's recognised motif. It is used universally in EU documents and on EU business. Grants of money are made for projects on the condition that a board carrying the flag is prominently displayed. The flag is used on every EU occasion, and member states are encouraged to use it too. It is regularly appearing on EU buildings, and increasingly on others as well. It now appears on number plates for vehicles and on passports. Flags are usually national symbols. Free trade does not need flags; countries always have a flag.

The twelve stars on the flag do not depict the member states, although there was a period during the development of the EU when, by coincidence, there were twelve members and twelve stars. They depict the twelve apostles, and are taken from a rose window in a Catholic church. They remind us of the Catholic and Holy Roman Empire origins of the idea of European union. It is no coincidence that Charlemagne's name has been attached to one of the principal EU buildings: he was a successful warrior emperor who extended imperial power.

The EU has an anthem, Beethoven's *Ode to Joy*, which is used on occasions when national anthems would normally be played. The name 'Union' is itself an interesting recent development. The grouping we joined, colloquially known as the Common Market here in Britain, was officially the European Economic Community. Many on the Continent, and especially in Brussels, used regularly to drop the word 'Economic', showing impatience with the Anglo-Saxon and the treaty view that this was only an economic or trading arrangement. This was endorsed by the member states in the Treaty of Maastricht, when the EEC was officially renamed the European Community, and when a wider-ranging purpose was incorporated for something called the European Union. The name and range of powers of the EU have been strengthened and given more prominence by the treaties of Amsterdam and Nice. The Community is now the Union, with responsibility for matters such as foreign policy, immigration and border controls, added by the three latest treaties. As the vetoes disappear, as a bigger corpus of legislation and court jurisdiction is ratified, so the EU ineluctably takes on the characteristics of a state.

Names, flags and anthems are symbols or indicators. Real power is exercised through legal rules and formal institutions. The EU has its own Supreme Court, the European Court of Justice (ECJ). It models itself on the American Supreme Court, a crucial agent in the expansion of federal power in the nineteenth century in the USA. Sir Patrick Neill has charted how the ECJ has operated in the last thirty years to expand the remit of European law and, above all, to establish the supremacy of European law over national law. In a series of pioneering judgements, the ECJ has now established – to its own satisfaction and to the satisfaction of many others, including many national courts – its right to be the court of final appeal in a wide range of cases. Even more importantly, it is well on the way to establishing the principle that it may overturn any Act or decision of any member states parliament, if it deems such an Act to be against the treaties. The Treaty of Nice added to the power of the courts, and established the supremacy of European Court decisions over any other form of law-making in the EU, short of an amendment to the founding treaties of the European Union. It laid down that all the courts in the member states are subservient to the European courts, and that they must follow the dictates of European law.

The EU is, first and foremost, a legal construction based on Continental-style law codes. The treaties themselves are expressed in looser and more straightforward language than much modern parliamentary legislation in Britain. They combine wide general statements of intent with specific measures and detailed provisions. The ECJ nearly always looks to the general intent of European integration when coming to its decisions, and construes the treaties in the direction of more European power. There is plenty of scope to do so, given how wide-ranging the treaty of European Union is.

The EU's tasks, the treaty makes clear, are to be carried out by the institutions – the European Parliament, the Council of Ministers, the Commission, the Court of Justice, the Court of First Instance, the Court of Auditors and the European Bank. Some believe it is possible to interpret this system as something different from a superstate in the making. They say that the main decisions are still taken by the Council of Ministers, with each national government separately represented. Some major issues are still settled by unanimity, so any state has a veto and can protect its own national interest. However, in recent years the erosion of the veto has been rapid, and even in a sensitive area such as taxation, where it is set to remain, the EU asserts more and more responsibility and influence, and takes more and more decisions. The Commission is there to help and carry out the wishes of the Council. The Parliament is still largely advisory, the Court is needed to enforce decisions. The proponents of this argument say that the European Union is different from a new country or state: it is more than a trading arrangement, it is a new concept.

Yet it seems clear from the progress of the treaties, the changes of name and, above all, the decisions being made by Commission and Court that it is easiest to understand the EU as a government in the making. A state claims allegiance from its citizens, it has a framework for their government, it develops policies in a wide range of areas. All this is true of the EU. The intention is to create a United States of Europe, with a Supreme Court, a Parliament or Congress, and, quite possibly in due course, an elected rather than a selected President. Could this ever work successfully?

There are few examples in history or in the present world where peoples speaking different languages are happy to live in the same state. Language divides people. It is difficult to support an effective democracy or accountable government if those governing cannot speak the language of some of those being governed. Misunderstandings and resentments build up. Those who speak different languages often also look at the world in different ways and have different customs.

Canada has shown how difficult it is to keep a bilingual democracy in being as a single country. Even though settlers went as volunteers to Canada many decades ago, and have been living together as one country for generations, the French and English speakers find it difficult to agree that Canada should remain a centralised, united single country. For some time, the French-speaking province of Quebec has been asserting its own identity. Its representatives in London, and elsewhere in the world, behave more like those of a national government than of a province or state in a federal union. There has been persistent pressure from many Quebecois either for more self-government, or to split altogether from the English-speaking provinces. Catalan separatism in Spain is connected with a different language. Irish independence was followed by a revival of Gaelic, with many official documents and letters offering some Gaelic as well as an English text. Most Welsh nationalists see their language as an important part of their identity, and a reason why Wales should be independently governed. The only success story for a multi-language country is the Swiss Federation, where cantonal government and limited federal government have worked for more than a century.

In western Europe, we are invited to believe that the eleven different national languages, to say nothing of the host of other languages and dialects, would not matter. But the EU already finds working in so many different languages a strain on its translation and other systems. Very often, the detailed working takes place in only two languages, French and English, and sometimes only a French text is available. This can be most frustrating for all those who are fluent in neither English nor French. There are occasions when nuances in meaning and tone are difficult to translate, leading to unintentional misunderstandings. Most people in western Europe speak, read and write only their own language: even after some years of compulsory second language teaching, most leave school uneasy at working or talking in a foreign language, a skill that soon deteriorates through lack of practice. It is unlikely that Europe will be any different from other places that have found keeping a single state together so difficult.

The United States was united around the English language as well as a single currency, the dollar. One of the entry requirements for immigrants was a rudimentary grasp of English. It was made clear to them that they would be expected to use English in every area of their lives. The Republican party is now alarmed by the rise of Spanish-speaking in the south, and is insisting on proper English education to reinforce the language as the cement of the Union. For a proper democratic debate to take place, with common ideas and disagreements, it is vital for participants to have a common language.

The single currency is part of this plan to create one country. The Republic of Ireland, although a fellow member of the EC with Britain, decided in the 1970s to establish its own currency and to drop the pound. This was a further illustration, if one were needed, that currency is seen as an important part of nationhood.

It is not just a question of symbols, although they are potent.

Over the centuries, monarchs and emperors have placed their images on coinage. Jesus said: "Render unto Caesar what is Caesar's" It is also a question of power. He who issues the banknotes may have a decisive influence on the state of the economy. As we will see in subsequent chapters, at the heart of the economic debates on the single currency lies the question of whether this economic power would be better or worse exercised by a Central European Bank than by national banks and parliaments.

The project to create a new country is breathtaking in the scale of its ambition. It encompasses up to 350 million people in fifteen different countries. The intention is to establish a federal government covering most important policies. It is difficult to conclude how the architects believe such a body could ever be truly accountable to its citizens, how it would establish legitimacy. The Germans feel that there should be a stronger European Parliament. They see it gradually gaining more power over the other Brussels institutions, although not over the Central Bank and economic policy. No one has ever suggested creating an elected western European government to take over from the unelected Commission and from the indirectly elected Council of Ministers. The only way there could be democratic control would be through pan-European elections to a proper parliament, with the government formed from the winning party or parties in the Parliament. No one designing the EU institutions intended Members of the European Parliament to wield any executive power. It is just a talking shop and sometimes, a rubber stamp for the Commission.

While the Germans would like to see the Parliament having a bigger say in passing new laws, there is as yet no proposal for such a parliament to become a directly taxing body or for it to replace the Council of Ministers. Various countries propose a steady erosion of individual country vetoes in the Council, and the further accretion of powers to the Parliament, but all have fallen short so far in clarifying where power lies by decisively favouring the Parliament. Pan-European parties are gradually emerging through coalition and common platform, between the two main groupings, the Christian democrats and the socialists. There is an implicit assumption that coalition politics is more likely than the winner-takes-all, two-party model of Britain, and that the powers of the constitution will be less clearly focused on a democratic assembly than we would like.

The lack of democratic accountability in the economic and monetary field is one of the most worrying features of the scheme. The European system's central banks, and especially the new European Central Bank at the heart of that system, are independent and very powerful. Their tasks are defined explicitly in the Maastricht treaty:

to define and implement the monetary policy of the Community; to conduct foreign exchange operations consistent with the provisions of Article 109 of this treaty; to hold and manage the official foreign reserves of the member states; to promote the smooth operation of payments systems.

Article 107 of the treaty explains just how independent they are to be:

When exercising the powers and carrying out the tasks and duties conferred upon them by this treaty and the Statute of the ESCB, neither the ECB, nor a national Central Bank, nor any member of their decision-making bodies shall seek or take instructions from Community institutions or bodies, from any government of a member state or from any other body. The Community institutions and bodies and the governments of the member states undertake to respect this principle and not to seek to influence the members of the decision-making bodies of the ECB or of the national central banks in the performance of their tasks.

The president, vice-president and other members of the executive board of the European Bank, by treaty, have to be appointed for an eight-year term, which cannot be renewed. These provisions are a bulwark to prevent any democratic influence at all over the monetary and currency policies being pursued by the European Bank.

Admirers of this scheme say that their very independence is vital to its success. It would be the triumph of technicians over politicians, of bankers over amateurs. The board has to be appointed 'from among persons of recognised standing and professional experience in monetary or banking matters by common accord of the Governments of the member states at the level of Heads of State or government, on a recommendation from the Council, after it has consulted the European Parliament, and the governing council of the ECB'.

Its apologists have in mind what they see as the great success of the German Central Bank in the post-Second-World-War era, which they believe has been based on the independence of that bank coupled with the pursuit of price stability as the prime aim.

Certainly they have designed a European system based on those two presumptions. Article 105 says that "the primary objective of ECB shall be to maintain price stability". No other policy objective will be allowed to interfere with the remit of zero inflation.

It is true that from 1945 to 1990 the German Central Bank had an excellent record for keeping inflation low compared with other western countries. It did not, however, succeed in running the German economy with zero inflation or 'price stability'. In practice, the European Central Bank has chosen to ignore the treaty requirement of price stability and zero inflation, and to opt for relatively low inflation, like the German Central Bank.

The German experience in the 1945-90 period was heavily influenced by the German experience of the 1920s, when Germany had the worst inflation record in the West. Germany experienced hyper-inflation, which wrecked her economy. We can still get an idea of what it must have been like when we look at German stamp and banknote collections, and the overprinting of values to try to keep up with the huge and rapid losses in the currency's worth. The new Germany after the war naturally wanted a currency and a constitution that made such a development unlikely to occur again. The reason the Central Bank in Germany was able to pursue a lower inflation policy than her neighbours was primarily because there existed in Germany a political consensus in favour of doing so. It was a matter of cross-party agreement, of common political thought, that Germany needed an independent Central Bank committed to low inflation.

Also, in the post-war period, the pursuit of low inflation did not conflict with other aims of German economic policy. Germany experienced a long and sustained boom as she emerged from the rubble of war. A ready supply of cheap labour from the east, and growing success in her education and training system for many native Germans, allowed her to create a strong economy based on the major industries of those days – engineering, steel and chemicals. The system worked: there was no need for the Central Bank to seek more permission or guidance from politicians.

All this changed markedly when the Berlin Wall came down, and when Europe started to move towards a single currency. The German Chancellor was desperate to reunite the two Germanys, even though the economy of the east was far behind the west in every way that mattered. Wages were lower. The supply and choice of consumer goods was restricted. The factories were antiquated, labour practices poor and machinery exhausted. East Germany was in no position to compete with the west on equal terms. The Central Bank advised against monetary union on favourable terms to East Germany, pointing out that it would be inflationary. If the bank had been truly independent, as many thought it was, that should have been an end to the matter. The Central Bank was right. It had spoken.

Instead, Chancellor Kohl ordered a currency and monetary union on terms favourable to the east – twice as favourable as the bank thought advisable. The predictable happened. Far too many extra DMs were created to replace the Ostmark, which was peremptorily abolished. East German savers were happy that they had more of a currency of some value. West Germans were horrified as the bills came in to rebuild the east. People in the east understandably wanted the same levels of wages and benefits as those in the west. Prices and wages soon escalated in East Germany as rebuilding, with federal money, began. Germany ended up with higher inflation than Britain and proved she did not have an independent Central Bank. When the politicians wanted to meddle with monetary policy, they could do so. The governor of the Central Bank, who had advised against merger, resigned.

The lack of independence was proved again over the issue of European currency union. Before the Maastricht Treaty was agreed, the German Central Bank advised that currency union with the rest of western Europe was not in Germany's interest. The Central Bank thought that whatever the treaty might say about the conduct of monetary policy and the characteristics of the new currency, it would be influenced by the more lax monetary policies of the other member states. The Central Bank echoed the fears of many Germans that the new currency would be less strong, less inflation-proof than the DM. Germany, said the bank, should stay with her national currency, and return to the ways of relative prudence that had characterised her monetary policy up to 1990. Again the bank was overruled, and Germany became the decisive founder member of the scheme. It is true that the warnings of the bank and many German people influenced the German stance on the European Bank. The bank was right to be worried that the new currency would be weak, for so it proved in its first two years. It is strange that people persist in viewing the German Central Bank as a model of independence, when it had to accept the abolition of the currency it was pledged to defend, even though it wanted to keep the DM!

The European Central Bank has decided that it is interested in the average rate of inflation for the EU, heavily influenced by the most populated countries at its heart, rather than the rates in the smaller peripheral countries such as Ireland and Portugal, where inflation is much higher. It has shown little sustained concern for the external value of the euro and no interest in creating price stability.

Monetary policy is widely agreed to be central in determining levels of prices and employment of resources, especially labour. Monetarist economists have concentrated on deducing from trends in the amount of money and credit in circulation the likely future levels of employment and prices. Their rivals, the Keynesians, look at somewhat different models of the economy, but in the work of their mentor, John Maynard Keynes, money plays a starring part. Keynes believed that money growth and the levels of government deficits or surpluses had an important impact on price and employment levels. The Maastricht Treaty gives sole control of money to the bank, and wishes to control the level of deficits of member states to help the bank with its task of controlling the rate of money growth. This means that the most important aspects of economic policy have been taken out of the hands of those elected by the democratic process and given to a committee of experts.

Some say this is a thoroughly good thing. They contrast the patchy record of economies where democratic politicians meddle with money, with an ideal of a perfect economy run by well-intentioned, successful experts free from base political interference. The only problem is, there is no example anywhere in the world of an economy made more successful by such a benign and independent form of regulation. In the post-war period, many Communists and fellow travellers argued that eastern Europe and the Soviet Union had wisely placed their economy in the hands of technocrats, central planners, free from democratic interference. But the result of that experiment was mass poverty in the centrally planned economies, and the highest living standards were to be found in the unruly, democratic USA. The Federal Reserve Board has operational independence, but it is usually run by someone who understands the political mood of Washington, and who regularly has to explain themselves to the legislature. It was noticeable that the Federal Reserve Board did not move interest rates during the sensitive run-up to the presidential election in 2000, nor for the following weeks when the outcome was still unclear, even though it was nervous about the slowdown in the economy. It looked as if they did not want to step into the political minefield of passing an opinion on the health of the economy until there was a political result because the economy was such an important issue in the campaign. As soon as it was clear that George Bush had won, they held an emergency meeting, cut interest rates, and subsequently changed policy to support tax cuts. This brought them into line with Republican thinking, and represented a U-turn from Democrat ideas that had prevailed throughout 2000.

If things go well, there is more chance of stability for the euro than if they do not. If, for example, a Europe with a single currency had unemployment of under 2 per cent, practically no inflation, an economic growth rate of 3 per cent with reasonable expectations of that continuing, and public spending growth of 2 per cent more than costs, then a political consensus would build around pursuing such a policy under the guidance of a powerful European Bank. Success might take the issue out of politics. My figures have not been chosen at random: my own constituency of Woking currently enjoys under 2 per cent unemployment, and is probably growing at 3 per cent a year, while British public spending is budgeted to rise by 2 per cent more than prices this year and next. This shows that it can be achieved in Europe.

The situation the bank inherited was very different. Unemployment is 10 per cent in France and 8 per cent in Germany. In Italy, it is 11 per cent, and in Spain 14 per cent. In recent years growth has been slower in Europe than in the USA. Should the world topple over into recession, these countries, still with high unemployment, would be required to cut their public spending to avoid excessive deficits, which might well cause them political anguish.

Unemployment rates, December 2000

Austria	4.6%
Belgium	8.2%
Denmark	5.2%
Finland	9.6%

cont'd . . .

France	9.7%
Germany	7.7%
Greece	11.4%
Ireland	4.2%
Italy	10.8%
Luxembourg	2.7%
Netherlands	2.8%
Portugal	4.1%
Spain	14.1%
Sweden	4.7%
UK	5.5%
Japan	4.7%
USA	4.0%

Some say that while the bank is powerful over money and currency policy, there is still action that member states' governments can take in response to the fears of their electors if the system does not immediately deliver a land of milk and honey. The government, they say, still has the power to settle public spending and tax rates. It can still offer grants and incentives to business or individuals.

It is true that, under the Maastricht Treaty, there is no explicit ban on a member state following a policy of low spending and low taxation, or of high spending and high taxation. What it cannot do, though, is follow a neo-Keynesian policy of high deficits to stimulate growth and jobs. Nor can it devalue its currency to make itself more competitive.

Some believe that a policy of low taxation stimulates industry and jobs. Indeed, all things being equal, I would say that is self-evidently true. A new firm setting up or an old firm expanding in

Europe – assuming that other things, such as the quality of the workforce, were broadly the same – would prefer to do so in a country where corporation tax was 25 per cent than where it was 50 per cent; would rather earn salaries where the top rate of tax was 40 per cent than where it was 60 per cent. While cutting tax rates stimulates growth and brings in more revenue from the extra activity, there is usually some loss of revenue to begin with. In a world of controlled deficits and low growth from tight monetary policies, countries would have to find expenditure cuts to pay for tax cuts. Experience has shown that most politicians find this difficult. The EU authorities are becoming concerned that some countries are stealing a march on others with lower tax rates. A committee has been established to try to put corporate taxes up to 'fairer' levels in the low-tax countries. The EU is also tightening its grip on taxation by other means – forcing the UK to adopt a turnover tax on art auction houses, preventing reductions in VAT, and expressing worries about cuts in vehicle excise duty.

Socialists believe that high tax-and-spend creates more jobs. This is possible under the Maastricht Treaty rules, but some of the spending with which socialists prefer to stimulate industry would not be permissible. Grants and subsidies to companies are likely to contravene the treaty, which rightly sees them as distortions in the market. While a socialist government could put up taxes and increase spending on health or welfare, it would have limited scope to increase spending on industrial or regional aid under treaty rules. Indeed, the UK government was blocked from offering money to BMW when it owned Rover, and in the other cases is finding it difficult to persuade it to give industrial aid to troubled areas.

There can be no single country called Europe and no single government that would attract the loyalty and support of the European peoples. Abolish the pound and you abolish an important part of Britain. You make a decisive move towards a country called Europe, governed from Brussels and Frankfurt.

The ten characteristics of a western nation state

1 It has its own name, anthem, flag and emblem.
2 It has a supreme court that controls all the other courts.
3 It has a parliament.
4 It has an executive government.
5 It has an army, navy and air force.
6 It has its own foreign policy.
7 It controls its own borders and decides who can and cannot enter.
8 It has its own currency.
9 It has a single market with common commercial laws.
10 It has its own criminal law code and system of justice.

How far has the European Union got in achieving these features of statehood?

1 It is called the European Union, and has its own flag, anthem and twelve-stars logo.
2 It has a Supreme Court, the European Court of Justice, which is confirmed as the only sovereign court in the member states by treaty.

3 It has a Parliament, which as yet has little power.

4 The Commission is the executive government of the EU, controlling most policy areas and making all new proposals for EU laws.

5 The EU is in the process of setting up Euroforce, to "project" its power abroad.

6 The EU has a single High Representative for its foreign policy, and is developing a common policy on most major international issues under the provisions of the treaty of Amsterdam. The EU handles negotiations on new international treaties for the member states in areas such as trade and the environment.

7 It has a common passport, is developing a common visa and borders policy, and has unified its frontiers for the Schengen group already.

8 The single currency comes into full use from 1 January 2002 in twelve member states.

9 It has a single market with common law codes.

10 It is well advanced in developing its own criminal justice system.

Chapter two

The EU will not stop wars; it wants an army to fight them

Europe has always been war-torn. Settled by different tribes over many centuries, several nations have attempted to conquer and plunder the others. Imperial Rome, the barbarian hordes, the Islamic armies, the Spanish, the French and the Germans, the Austrians, the Russians and the Turks have all had their ambitions. Sometimes these great powers have acted out of fear: fear for their own borders, fear that they are being encircled by others. Sometimes they have acted aggressively, believing that Europe would be better if it were more united under their direction. All these efforts at creating a European empire have failed, usually because a coalition of other states have emerged to resist and ultimately overthrow the aggressor.

The most common argument for European integration – and therefore for the single currency – is that a more integrated western Europe will prevent such wars breaking out. This is reminiscent of the idealism at the end of the First World War: many believed, or wanted to believe, that it had been the war to end all wars. We must ask ourselves if it is likely that strengthening government in Brussels and Frankfurt for up to fifteen countries in western Europe – or for twenty-seven countries across Europe, once the enlargement of the EU has taken place – can bring about the permanent peace we would all like.

The presence of the EU as a force on the world stage did not prevent war in Yugoslavia. Indeed, the combined efforts of EU countries probably exacerbated and prolonged it, from when Germany, and in effect the rest of us, first recognised Croatia as a separate country to when the USA intervened to assist our over-committed forces and impose some kind of settlement.

As always with European matters, this has led to rows over how we should interpret these events. Some of us conclude that NATO and the UN are the right international bodies to handle such problems, and that the intervention of the EU served only to complicate and worsen a bad situation. Others feel that we need a stronger EU with a European army at the ready to intervene more extensively than the French and British armies did in Bosnia or could have done in Kosovo. The British army performed valiantly, but had to operate under ambiguous instructions from the UN and EU.

In the closing months of 2000, the argument about a common army for Europe came to the fore. It has long been the ambition of France that European forces should be detatched, in part, from NATO. France wants to create a European force that operates independently of the USA and has its own sphere of influence. Germany is attracted to the idea of combined forces, as she throws off the legacy of the Second World War and looks for an acceptable way of using her own forces in a common cause outside her borders.

The British Prime Minister, Tony Blair, decided that here was an initiative in which the UK could play a leading role. Blocked by public opinion from putting forward British membership of the euro, he wanted to offer proof to our partners that Britain under a Labour government was committed to a more integrated Europe. He proposed a common force. Soon it emerged that France had trumped him, going further than sceptical British opinion would allow, and further than the US administration wanted.

The USA made encouraging noises, not wanting to upset her European allies. She wanted to encourage the EU to make a bigger contribution to the combined global forces of NATO in general, and to take on more of the responsibility for military activity in Europe in particular. The USA was reluctant to become involved in the Balkans, but had to help when her European allies found they had bitten off more than they could chew. When the USA discovered that the EU force would take troops, planes and ships currently pledged to NATO and use them under a different command in places and operations with which NATO had not agreed, she sounded warning bells.

It is difficult to see how a stronger EU could prevent wars in the most unsettled parts of our continent. The war in the south of Russia goes on unaffected by European integration. Conflict is always possible in the east as those countries emerging from the collapsing Soviet empire seek to establish their identity and fair boundaries. As the EU regards strengthening central control as more important than widening the number of countries in its remit, it is expressly implying that creating a strong state in western Europe is more important to it than trying to help

43

stabilise the more unsettled east. One of the extraordinary features of the Nice Treaty was that the UK government and others tried to tell us that this was essential to enlargement, when most of the issues it covered were essential to further centralisation of the existing fifteen members. The most difficult issue for enlargement, reform of the common agricultural policy, was not tackled at all. Only the clauses on voting rights and the number of Commissioners were directly related to the possible future inclusion of new states.

The EU plan for a combined force offers no hope of resolving the conflict between Greece and Turkey, no obvious solution to the question of how far the borders of the new Russia should stretch, no clear view on the relationship between Hungary and Romania or on the borders of states east of the river Elbe.

My main concern is with Britain. Our country has been involved in all too many European wars over the last two thousand years. We were conquered twice by Continental aggression: first by the Romans, and then by the Normans. In the first millennium, Danes and Norwegians raided and settled. Since 1066, we have recognised that we are a European country by geography, history, interest and inclination. We have fought to prevent Spanish, French and German domination of the Continent. Although we have enjoyed obvious advantages from our island position off the north-western coast of the mainland, our history has been interwoven with that of the main Continental countries.

There have been times when we have been the aggressor. In the Middle Ages, England asserted and often enforced territorial claims to parts of France, especially to Aquitaine and the Calais region. These were dropped in the sixteenth century and have never been revived. In the second half of the second millennium, we have fought for colonies that other European countries had claimed, in the interests of widening our commercial and territorial empire.

There is no need for and no likelihood of future wars based on British aggression. We do not seek new colonies or covet other people's territory. We now have largely settled frontiers, and have long since given up the idea that we should have more territory on the Continent. No Continental power has recently disputed our rights to the British Isles, excluding the Republic of Ireland. There are no claims for the Isle of Wight or the Isles of Scilly. France accepts that the Channel Islands are Crown territories, with a substantial amount of self-government, outside the EU. The only remaining issue over frontiers between ourselves and a Continental country lies with our ownership of Gibraltar.

Spanish claims to Gibraltar often disrupt EU meetings. The EU has proved no more adept at resolving the dispute than the antagonists. As far as Britain is concerned, Gibraltar is British, and should remain so. That is the wish of the people there, and it is ours by long practice. To say it is Spanish because it is close to Spain is as sensible as saying the Republic of Ireland is British because it is close to Britain and was once part of the UK. This should not become a cause of war between Britain and Spain, with or without the EU handling foreign policy. As long as Gibraltarians want to remain British, and as long as we show resolve in wanting the Rock to be British, the Spanish will realise that they cannot succeed diplomatically or militarily.

In the sixteenth and seventeenth centuries, England stood against Spanish domination of the Low Countries and much else. Spain wished to impose a Catholic settlement over Anglican England and Presbyterian Scotland, as well as over Lutheran and Calvinistic communities in Holland and Belgium. A Continental exclusive system of religion was to be forced on countries and people who favoured a more tolerant style. England was of critical importance in leading the resistance to such tyranny.

A more common cause of wars between the UK and some of her neighbours has been our wish to stop any single European country gaining hegemony over the Continent. Britain has always felt her interests threatened if those parts of the Continent closest to us fall under the control of a single nation. Napoleon showed us why this would be a bad idea from the British point of view: he aimed to impose a Continental system that excluded British goods and services from Continental markets, ushering in a protectionist regime orchestrated in the interests of France. Britain had to resist, and find coalition partners who would help to take on the might of France.

In the twentieth century, the UK, with the USA, twice had to stand firm against German domination of the Continent. The Hitlerian scheme was for a Europe united under German influence or control, with a single European economy and currency to be imposed after a successful conclusion of the war. The mass genocide of the Jews and the scorn for democracy were but two of the many horrible features of these plans, which rightly led the western democracies to fight.

How likely is such imperialism to reappear, and would membership of a more centralised EU prevent it? Here I am an optimist: I do not believe that the four large western European Continental countries harbour military and imperial ambitions. Of course, Holland, Belgium, Denmark and Luxembourg have no intention of invading their far more powerful neighbours to establish themselves as the imperial power. Neither do I see evidence of this in Spain or Italy.

If you press enthusiasts for a country called Europe to clarify how it might prevent war, they will often agree with what I have written so far. To them, the advantage comes from ensuring that France and Germany will not go to war again. I find it surprising that they have so little confidence in democratic Germany and France that they think either might declare war on the other. I also find it difficult to understand how the Brussels institutions would stop them if they wished to do so.

However, I do think the current plans for European union are likely to cause greater tensions between countries and peoples in western Europe. It is especially worrying that enthusiasts for union hold the USA as their example. They say that the common market of the USA needed a single currency and a single government to unite it and create its prosperity, and that Europe needs the same.

History tells us a different story. The USA came into existence through a war against Britain. It gained a sense of identity and community through the war of independence, throwing off

British government control. It fought a war against Mexico to gain territory in the south. As the nineteenth century continued, the differences in style, attitude and social systems between the southern and northern states polarised them. The election of Lincoln, a northerner, as President, led directly to a bitter, bloody civil war. The issue was the power of the individual member states: the southern states claimed the right to secede from the union and conduct their own affairs; the northern states said they must recognise the higher power of the federal institutions. The federal power won, because it was backed by the industrial and military might of the northern states. During the course of the conflict, the issue of slavery became important, but it was comparatively late on that Lincoln declared against slavery for the USA and it was not the cause of the war.

This is not a prepossessing model for a United States of Europe. Europe has none of the advantages the USA had in its formation. The states of western Europe do not have to unite to throw off some colonial power. Those who migrated to the USA wanted something different: they disliked the countries and cultures they were leaving, and sought a better life. They volunteered to become Americans. Most of us in western Europe are not trying to leave behind our own culture and identity or change the way in which we are governed.

New arrivals in the USA were asked to swear allegiance to the USA. They were required to learn English, the common language, and were happy to accept the dollar, the common currency. Despite all this, they entered an horrendous civil war before they established their federal destiny.

Would a deeper union make war between Germany and France impossible? No. It would make a future war different: it would be a war about states rights, or it might take the form of an insurrection against the federal power, but at root it might still be a war between the French and German ways of doing things. The best guarantee of no more wars between France and Germany lies in both countries remaining prosperous democracies, in which their governments and peoples see no advantage in going to war. This has been the position since 1945, without a political union between the two countries. It has also helped that the USA, Britain and other well-armed allies are interested in a peaceful future for Europe. NATO has kept the peace since the war, although Germany was divided and occupied by allied armies for the first forty-five years afterwards, just to make sure, but democratic Germany has welcomed peace. No western European power has wanted to grab territory from a neighbour, but if it had, NATO forces would have discouraged it.

The argument that deeper political union would stop war pulls the heart-strings. There is enough first-hand memory of the world wars of the twentieth century for the peoples of western Europe rightly to fear another. It is not political union that will prevent future wars, but a community of interest between differing peoples, and/or enough force ranged on the side of peace. For more than fifty years Europe has proved that this method works

The Franco-German relationship has become the crucial relationship in European politics. For most of the post-war years, France found it easy to lead the relationship: Germany was rehabilitating herself politically, and West Germany alone was not disproportionately large. The merger of the two Germanys has changed that: now France shows signs of schizophrenia and fear. On the one hand, she throws her weight around by testing nuclear weapons, reminding Germany and the rest of the world that she has an independent nuclear force and is more powerful militarily than Germany. On the other hand, in the 1990s, when it came to the future of Europe, successive French leaders took their orders or direction from Chancellor Kohl. More recently, President Chirac has found that Germany can flex her muscles when France presses too hard on their friendship and alliance. In December 2000 at Nice, France set out her view of a more centralised EU with the two main powers, France and Germany, given a stronger position to run it together. Chancellor Schroeder disagreed, and the press took it as a sign that Germany will now dominate the alliance in public as well as in private.

France struggles desperately to keep in the running for monetary and political union, whatever the cost in lost jobs and lost opportunities. She accepts the need to merge much of her country's government with Germany, as if Germany posed an immediate threat to her.

I remember asking a leading French politician once how she could believe that France would direct Germany and Europe in the era after the Berlin Wall came down. She replied that she knew in her heart that France could not, but she could not think of an alternative to the policy they were following. The French have traditionally been a proud and independent nation: they will not take kindly to their independence being squandered, if it does not bring many benefits. French men and women have already taken to the streets in protest against the economic policies being followed in the name of monetary union.

Germany is becoming more bombastic. Since the wall came down and she was reunited, her centre of gravity has shifted eastwards, and her sense of her own power and influence has changed noticeably. Germany is a larger country than the other big three in western Europe: France, the UK and Italy all have between 55 and 60 million citizens; the new Germany has 80 million. Although, on average, Germany's living standards are now similar to those of the other three, her total national output is around a third higher because of the extra people. The years of German engineering and manufacturing success and excellence in the 1970s and early 1980s have also left their legacy: other European countries think Germany is stronger than she is. With France prepared to acquiesce to the German plan, Britain undecided about closer union and Italy finding it difficult to establish a stable government, Germany has a relatively easy task in asserting her view of European developments.

As the political union develops, so common defence forces and a united foreign policy become more important. The EU has appointed a High Representative or foreign policy supremo to speak for the EU in foreign affairs. The French want his or her statements to be backed by a European army within a few months to give teeth to what is said on behalf of the fifteen member states. What guarantee is there that this would prevent wars rather than create new ones? Presumably an armed EU would take an interest in the conflicts of its members. Would such a union agree to take the Greek side in any argument with Turkey? Will the EU continue to favour Croatia against Serbia? How far might the EU go in asserting its view of how the whole Balkan area should be settled? What would the EU's view be in any border disputes affecting Poland, Hungary and Romania? Would the EU take the side of the Sudetenland Germans, who believe the lands in the Czech Republic that they acquired in the 1930s and lost at the end of the war should be restored? How would the EU develop its relationship with Russia? Is it happy to allow Russia to do as she wishes in Chechnya? What if Russia changed her policy towards Estonia, Latvia and Lithuania? Would the EU object? If Algerian and other north African immigration remains a problem for the Mediterranean areas of the EU, will the EU have to take a stronger line on these matters? Will the EU take a different view of the Arab-Israeli conflict from that taken by the USA?

The EU of the fifteen states has large, difficult borders. Beyond them lie a number of small, fragile, unstable countries. Can we be sure that an armed EU with a single foreign policy will help in each of these cases? Might not some of our neighbours find such a development alarming? Isn't it possible that Britain would get dragged into conflicts far from home that might not otherwise trouble her?

The emerging common foreign policy might become a source of tension between member states, and between individual member states and the EU. Either Spain or Britain will be disappointed when EU policy determines who should control Gibraltar. Greece will be disappointed if the union will not back her in all her arguments with Turkey. France will be unhappy if the attitude to Algeria is not the one she would like. Italy is concerned about the Balkans policy, which has not created the stability that she would like in her neighbours.

Monetary union has to be seen against this bigger political backdrop. It is part of the jigsaw of the new Europe – an important part, but only part of a huge plan to create a country called Europe. Those who debate it as an economic issue do a grave injustice to the vision of those who wish to bring it about. The idea behind currency union is to lock the economies of western Europe into one. It began with the European Coal and Steel Community, bringing together the big industries that had fuelled the war machines of the main countries, France and Germany, in the first half of the century. It is now developing, with the idea of uniting the economies as a whole as one. It means one weapons industry, one steel and coal industry, one set of rules, one political purpose. A single economic policy would entail a major move towards one government. The ultimate aim is full political union.

The argument that all this would mark an end to wars on our continent is simply untrue. The presence of the enlarged EC trying to work together in foreign policy as elsewhere has not stopped wars in the 1990s in Europe. It has not stopped civil strife from the Irish Nationalists, the Basque separatists or the African protesters in Paris. It has not stopped war in the Balkans or in the former Soviet empire. It is very much in Britain's interest to keep the peace, and to keep the arteries of trade unclogged. It has been in the interests of neither France nor Germany to go to war in the second half of the twentieth century. There is no reason for them to do so in the future, and there is NATO and US power as the ultimate guarantors of the peace. Far from making war less likely, a stronger European union might make disagreement and conflict, if not war, more likely. It adds another power to a complicated equation, before the issue of states rights has been properly resolved.

The early days of the European army have not been encouraging to those of us who believe that NATO is the prime force for the defence of liberty and democracy. The French want the army to be controlled separately from NATO, with separate intelligence, and to operate where and when NATO does not wish to be engaged. The British idea that it should be an adjunct of NATO, sharing intelligence with NATO and helping in areas and conflicts where NATO is happy that it should do so, is losing out to the more aggressive position of the French government. The plan already encompasses an EU Military Committee, an EU Political Committee to direct it, and big investment in separate intelligence command and control so it can be independent of NATO.

Ten fears of a euro army

1 A proper European army is not under NATO command. It will start to distance the USA from the defence of western Europe.

2 The European army does not have the back-up of the American heavy lift, needed to get troops and equipment in

and out in a hurry, or the naval and missile back-up of the US forces: meaning it will be more vulnerable than NATO-backed troops.

3 The European army will break intelligence links with the USA, vital links for the well-being and success of our forces.

4 The European army, navy and air force is designed to undertake operations that NATO is not prepared to support. What are these wars and missions we want to undertake with which NATO does not agree?

5 The development of a European army worries the eastern countries not in the EU. They do not see it as a stabilising force.

6 The European army may well intervene in places where it cannot create peace and stability, such as the Balkans. It will over-commit our forces, as the EU tasks are in addition to home defence and our NATO commitments.

7 An EU army will pull loyalties apart. Are we British or European? Can our soldiers be loyal to the EU and carry out its wishes?

8 Is there any intention or danger of a European army being used for internal purposes within the EU if opposition builds up?

9 It will cause tensions with the USA, our main ally, as the European army will be deployed in actions in which the USA does not wish to involve itself and with which it may disagree. It will increasingly create tension between the two supply industries, European and American, and may limit our access to US technology.

10 Once majority voting is in place for defence and foreign policy, British soldiers might be sent to fight wars against which Britain voted, but was overruled.

Chapter three

A Europe of the regions; devolution does not work

The argument for monetary union has become part and parcel of the argument about a Europe of the regions. It was put vividly by Umberto Bossi, the self-appointed leader of the North Italian League. In September 1996, Signor Bossi led a demonstration across northern Italy and sailed into Venice to declare a northern Italian state. Proclaiming the need for a new country called Padania, stretching from Turin to Venice along the Po valley, he made clear that he was a fan of the idea of a Europe of the regions. In the name of such a Europe, he rejected the authority of the central Italian government, demanded a self-governing Padania and welcomed further moves to European integration.

There is a similar gleam in the eye of the Catalan leadership in eastern Spain. They, too, would like looser links with Madrid or independence for Catalonia from the Spanish monarchy and Parliament. They, too, welcome the idea of a Europe of the regions, seeing in the European ideal a way to demolish the powers of the Spanish state.

In the UK, a minority of Scots take the secessionist line. They wish to divorce Scotland from the rule of London and see in the concept of a Europe of the regions a device to help them in their cause against British power.

The unholy alliance between Brussels and these separatist movements is one that cannot last indefinitely. For the moment, it is a marriage of convenience: the Brussels authorities and the regional movements have a common cause: to weaken or demolish central authority in the nation states of western Europe. What will become apparent as they proceed is the fundamental incompatibility of those who believe that even a nation state is too large to govern them sensibly with those who wish to create a new nation state on the scale of the whole of western Europe.

The claims of the Italian separatists in northern Italy are both economic and political. They see the connection between the two. Northern Italy feels that southern Italy drags it down. At a time of economic failure with high unemployment across Italy, the problems are acute in the south. As a result, in the unified state called Italy, the north has to pay higher taxes to support the south and make up for its higher level of unemployment. This causes economic resentments.

In Spain, there has been a long tradition of unity, but it has always been based on the distinctive identity of each principal region. Catalonia was once a separate kingdom. It still uses a different language and has always seen itself as the most prosperous, bustling and commercial part of Spain. Barcelona is Spain's first city, if this was measured by commercial and trading importance. There has always been a strong rivalry between Barcelona and Madrid over how much government should come from the centre and how much should be left to Catalonia. The Spanish crisis has deepened with every step Spain has taken in recent years to try to bring her economy into line with Germany's in preparation for monetary union. Starting from much lower levels of real income, productivity and technology, she has been through a rapid process of modernisation. Now she is strained by the strict monetary requirements on debt, government deficits, inflation and interest rates. Spain found it difficult to keep to EU economic rules, and in so doing, precipitated a sharp decline in her economy. She is now burdened with 14 per cent unemployment, and young people, in particular, lack jobs. Unrest about the state of an economy is easily channelled into demands for regional separatism. An old Spanish rhyme from the sixteenth century says the New World was given by Christopher Columbus to Castile.

A Castil y a Leon
Nuevo mundo dio Colon . . .

It was always felt that the heart of Spain was Castile and Leon. The Basque country to the north-east and Catalonia to the east always felt somewhat distanced from the central core clustering around the court and monarchy.

The Spanish kingdom was united through its reconquest from the Moors. Disparate regions – Extremadura, Galicia, Granada, Castilla, Catalonia, Murcia and Asturia – were welded together, united by one religion, Christianity, one currency based on gold and one monarchy. A federal structure was designed for parliamentary representation in the Cortes, but a strong sense of

59

regional identity persisted. Separatist feeling was least pronounced when Spanish power and influence globally was at its peak, but became more pronounced as the achievement of the Spanish kingdom waned in the nineteenth and twentieth centuries.

Similar feelings of regionalism have been present within the UK. While England has been, largely happy with its status as a single national entity within the UK, there have been endless arguments and debates about the role of Scotland, Ireland and, to a lesser extent, Wales within it. England herself has long been united under one crown with a single currency, the Christian religion and common governmental institutions. A common system of justice, parliamentary representation and local goverment has been in existence for many centuries. There are no rumblings of Northumbrian or Wessex nationalism. While people are dimly aware that more than a thousand years ago there were separate kingdoms in the country now called England, they do not yearn to return to them.

Nor are there strong rumblings for Welsh separatism. Wales has been part of the combined kingdom for more than five hundred years. It was finally brought into alliance and union with England when a successful Welsh dynasty took the combined throne. While it is true that a minority of the Welsh hanker after a former time when Wales was ruled by its own princes, this has never amounted to more than a fifth of the popular vote, and many of those who have nationalist inclinations would fall short of recommending the complete separation of Wales from England under its own independent government.

When a lesser scheme of devolution was proposed in the 1970s, suggesting an assembly in Wales to deal with Welsh issues under the sovereignty of the British Parliament, even this was rejected decisively by the electorate. When the new Labour government came to power in the UK in 1997 it offered the Welsh another chance to set up an assembly to give some voice to Wales as a political nation. Only a quarter of the population bothered to vote in favour, carrying the day by a narrow margin. The early days of the assembly were dogged by the Westminster Labour government's insistence on choosing the leader and dictating policy, even though the Labour Party had failed to secure an overall majority in the assembly. Since the Welsh Labour Party cut free and chose its own leader, the assembly has proved an ineffective talking shop that has made little visible difference to the government of Wales, apart from spending more money on politicians and bureaucrats.

Scotland came into complete union with England and Wales in 1707. In 1603, the union of crowns took place with the accession of the Scottish King James VI who, as Elizabeth I's heir became James I of England. As with the Welsh, so with the Scots. A Scottish king therefore made the historic decision to come to London and govern from there: he saw the potential of the combined kingdom in European and international politics. It was a Scottish government that agreed in 1707 to a union of the parliaments and to most of the important powers of Scottish government passing to the sovereign Parliament in London.

Despite the legacy of goodwill that the Scottish takeover of England created in Scotland, and despite the obvious advantages of the combined kingdom to the Scottish people, particularly during the period of imperial success in the nineteenth and early twentieth centuries, in recent years there has been a stronger movement in Scotland against the current style of union. There is still nothing like a majority of Scottish people who would like to see an entirely separate Scotland. In general elections, Scottish Nationalists typically win three or four seats out of seventy-two in total; and in any case, their manifestos usually fall short of demanding a complete separation of the two countries. When the issue of a devolved assembly was put to the Scottish people at the end of the 1970s, a small majority of those voting favoured more devolved government in Scotland. However, because they did not constitute an overall majority of the Scottish people, the matter was not carried. That many Scots refrained from voting indicated that the issue was not then of burning concern to the majority. In the 1990s, the mood changed. After 1997, the new Labour government recognised this and offered another referendum on devolution. There was considerable enthusiasm for a Scottish Parliament, which was voted in by a substantial majority. The early days of the Parliament have not impressed many Scots. Nationalists see it as a first step on the way to full governing power. Unionists hope it will calm tempers, but so far nothing significant has changed or improved, and the Parliament has been dogged by conflicts and arguments about sleaze.

Ireland has been the most difficult area of the UK. A long and bitter history of conflict between Catholics and Protestants continues to this day. In the early twentieth century, this manifested itself as a Catholic Nationalist rising against membership of the UK, which led, after the end of the First World War, to the creation of a separate Republic of Ireland. Today, some of the Catholics in Northern Ireland favour incorporation into the Republic while other Catholics and practically all Protestants in the north wish to remain part of the UK. The immediacy of the conflict over identity encourages stronger and more extrovert British nationalism in the Protestant community in Northern Ireland than is usually seen among the English on the mainland. The threat to their presence in the UK makes them its staunch defenders. The UK government has made clear that while a majority of the Ulster people wish to remain in the UK they will do so. This does not meet with the approval of radical Nationalists who want to reunite Ireland.

The conclusion I come to is that the union of the UK, although there are dissenters, remains the best way of organising the government of its different countries and regions. It is a democratic union. If any part of it developed a strong majority view that they would be better off outside it, a political way would be found to bring it about peacefully. The deep roots of the union through history account for its vitality and strength. Britain is the best example of a stable, integrated, successful country in the whole of western Europe. The UK lays claim to be one of a small group of relatively peaceful and stable countries. France was convulsed by revolution only two hundred years ago. Both Germany and Italy came together as countries only in the nineteenth century, and have both undergone periods of Fascist tyranny during the twentieth. Spain is only just recovering from Fascism and a twentieth-century civil war. Belgium is a deeply divided country between its Flemish- and French-speaking parts. Luxembourg is small enough for no further divisions to be possible, and Holland's unity comes from having thrown off Spanish and Hapsburg domination in the sixteenth century, reinforced by the country`s Protestant religion.

It would be possible to build separatist and regional movements in many of these countries. In Spain, the Catalan movement is already well under way. In Spain and France, the Basques have for many years campaigned and even resorted to terrorism to try to create a separate country. In Belgium, many would like to see two jurisdictions rather than one and in Germany the pull of the different parts is quite strong, with Brandenberg Prussia being very different in tone and feel from Bavaria or the western regions.

Those who favour the single currency often view regional movements as their natural allies. This is to play with fire. We have seen an extreme example of what can happen in the former Yugoslavia. When the central communist control was removed, people debated not only a transition to democratic government, but also how big an area that democratic government should control. The rival claims of Serbia, Croatia and Bosnia were all heard loud and clear. Yugoslavia began to split apart. It emerged that it was difficult to create a natural democracy that all the different religions and ethnic groups would regard as satisfactory. Yugoslavia split into a Serbia, a Croatia and a Bosnia. In Bosnian elections, the electorate said they felt Bosnia in turn should split into three, as each group felt it could not get justice or a satisfactory government by belonging to Bosnia as a whole.

A long and bitter civil war has ensued following the collapse of central Yugoslavian authority. The tensions between Serbs and Kosovans boiled over into a bruising civil war. It has not made people turn to over-arching solutions of a united Balkans in an effort to modernise and recreate the Austrian Hapsburg empire. On the contrary, it has led people to demand ever smaller units of government.

Exponents of the single currency argue that these regional passions are there and cannot be suppressed. They see the regional passions as their natural allies in helping them to destroy the authority and legitimacy of national government. They then believe that belonging to such small countries, people would naturally turn to the Frankfurt Central Bank and to the European single currency to provide the unifying economic policy and the common coinage. I think they will be bitterly disappointed if they do pursue this very dangerous route. The same forces that encouraged Umberto Bossi in northern Italy to reject the authority of Rome would lead his successors to reject the authority of Brussels and Frankfurt. The main worry northern Italians have is that they are paying too high a price for their union with the south. It is northern companies' profits and northern workers' wages that are raided by the taxman in order to cross-subsidise the expensive south. If northern Italy were part of the European currency union, far from losing that burden, it would gain new burdens with obligations to other regions in other former countries of western Europe. We must presume for these purposes that the southern Italy rump would apply for currency membership as well. Northern Italy would still, therefore, be in the same economic policy area, indeed in the same country, as southern Italy, but the country would now be called Europe rather than Italy. The problem would remain.

Southern Italy will continue to perform less well than northern Italy. Indeed, sharing an economic policy with Germany as well as with northern Italy might make the problem worse, exacerbating the tight money and high unemployment policies that have characterised recent Italian and German experience. Far from lessening the burden of support, it may increase the burden of support from northern Italy to southern Italy. On top of that, the more successful northern Italy would have to accept responsibilities towards eastern Germany, north-eastern France and other poorer parts of the currency union.

Creating a sense of nationhood is not the same as encouraging a crude nationalism that can be damaging to neighbours. A sense of nationhood means that people living in that country accept mutual responsibilities and obligations. A citizen of a nation or a subject of a monarchy accepts the rule of law of that country, participates in the common institutions to establish and uphold the law and accepts financial obligations to other members of that country's community. As a southern Englishman who believes in the United Kingdom, I fully accept British law. I accept British law even though it is now determined by a Labour government with a preponderance of Scottish, Welsh and northern English MPs and Scottish ministers in key positions. I accept the legitimacy of the system. I enjoy the freedom to oppose them and to seek to persuade the British people that it is better to elect a different type of government. When the Conservative Party lost in 1974, I campaigned for a future victory in a future election. I did not urge disobedience of the law or a change in the system. After defeat in 1997, I did not oppose a Labour government because there were so many Scottish members of the Cabinet. They had every right to be there. I opposed what they did, not where they came from.

Similarly, as a southern Englishman I accept that because my part of southern England is relatively more successful and prosperous than other parts of the UK, it is reasonable that we should pay more in tax so that there can be a decent level of benefits and support to people in parts of the country that are now prospering less well. I am quite happy at the thought that I will pay tax in order to help a blind person in Liverpool or an unemployed person in Glasgow. The sense of nationhood binds us together and we accept mutual obligations.

Such a sense of accountability and acceptance takes many centuries to nurture and bring to fruition. As we have seen in England, it has developed over a thousand years and in the UK over three hundred. I would not feel a similar sense of loyalty or sense of mutual obligation to people in Leipzig or Dresden or Calais or Sicily. If someone said to me that I should obey laws which had been primarily determined by elected members from Continental countries, I would disagree. I would want to change the system that perpetrated such an outrage. Similarly, if by virtue of a currency union people said I then had to accept obligations to pay higher taxes to look after unemployed young people in Sicily, or women on maternity leave in France, I would disagree. I do not have that sense of nationhood and shared purpose that I feel with fellow citizens in the UK.

It is possible to have a strong sense of local or regional identity and a strong sense of nationhood. Many Welshmen are extremely proud to be Welsh. They express their Welsh feelings in pride in language, history, culture and achievement. They are also proud of the UK and share a common pride in the buildings and institutions of London as of Cardiff. Both work because both are based on a long history and evolution. It would be difficult to hold an equivalent loyalty to three levels: Wales, the UK and Europe. Those who favour a stronger sense of European identity in Wales are usually the same people who favour more or less radical change in the UK, leading to a reduction of national power.

The single-currency scheme, if brought into being, could increase the sense of regional frustration rather than allay it. What begins as an alliance between regionalism and federalism soon deteriorates into a bitter conflict. The people of northern Italy would find they had to pay bigger contributions to the poorer parts of the union than they do to their current Italian union; they might also find that the economic policy being pursued by the Frankfurt Central Bank was even more hostile to their economic interests than are the policies currently being pursued by the Italian government. True regional separatists should say 'No' to Brussels as well as to Rome.

The European Community is trying to counter this problem by encouraging a different approach to economic management. They are going round spending money and time on encouraging a sense of regional identity. In my own part of southern England, they are trying to persuade us that we should have both a south-eastern regional identity and a Thames Valley identity. Neither of these makes much sense. Their south-eastern region excludes London, yet London lies at the heart of the south-eastern region. If you ask people to define the Thames Valley, even those of us who live in it would have great difficulty in defining its boundaries or borders. The Thames Valley is a geographical, not a political, fact of life. We understand Berkshire, Oxfordshire, Hampshire. These are longstanding counties that have been reflected in local government, the dispensation of justice, in cricket teams and road signs. We do not, at the moment, have any sense of south-eastern identity excluding London, and little sense of an economic region called the Thames Valley.

One propoganda booklet printed for the European Commission to give the south-east a sense of regional identity delves into history to establish European connections. We are told 'Roman and Norman links are evident across the sub-region to show that the ties with Europe stretch far back into history'. There is no explanation that these 'links' were the result of invasion and military settlement – hardly a good way to encourage a sense of European togetherness.

The EC thinks it can make regions out of a few leaflet drops, brochures and grant programmes. The brochure seems almost to regret that it is by and large a prosperous area, but cheers up when it finds pockets of unemployment and deprivation that can be touched by Eurogrants. The deeper motive oozes from every sentence: the EC wants to undermine the nation in order to build a bigger one.

Ten things wrong with devolution

1 Scottish and Welsh nationalists are not happy; they do not think devolution goes far enough.

2 Scottish and Welsh unionists are not happy; they think it goes too far and will drive a wedge between the parts of the union.

3 The UK government has not been happy; it thought the wrong people were elected!

4 This type of devolution makes government bigger and dearer; there are more politicians and bureaucrats administering the same services.

5 Lop-sided devolution leaves the problem of England unsolved. Welsh and Scottish MPs at Westminster can vote on English issues, but cannot vote on most Scottish and Welsh matters. English MPs cannot vote on Scottish or Welsh matters.

6 It has created two types of MP at Westminster. English MPs handle the whole range of issues, but Scottish MPs cannot handle planning, transport, law and order, local government, health, the environment or most other things of immediate interest to their constituents. What do Scottish MPs do all day?

7 Proportional representation means no party wins outright and no one is to blame. It makes it more difficult for electors to know how to get problems solved.

8 The blurred responsibilities between Whitehall and the devolved administrations also make it impossible for voters to know who has done what. When farmers are suffering as

they are, is the EU to blame (responsible for the common agricultural policy), or Whitehall (responsible for national regulation), or the devolved administration (responsible for local agricultural matters)? It usually means no-one takes responsibility and there is no answer for the farmers.

9   Devolution tends to exacerbate racial and linguistic tensions, by stressing differences rather than similarities.

10 Scottish and Welsh nationalists say they want more European integration, but at a certain point they will come to dislike Brussels government as much as they currently dislike London administration.

Chapter four

Problems with rigged exchange rates

The Exchange Rate Mechanism is a device to keep the European currencies in line with one another, to try to smooth out the normal fluctuations in exchange rates. Joining the Exchange Rate Mechanism and keeping a stable rate within it for two years is an essential pre-condition, as outlined in the Maastricht treaty, for any country wishing to join the single currency. The original scheme designed at Maastricht goes back to earlier visions of how a single currency should be brought about. It was always assumed that it would take place by pegging currencies one to another in an exchange-rate grid or snake. Over time, the authorities would reduce the permitted variations until it was a relatively straight-forward step to replace all the different member-state currencies with the single common currency or the ECU, a basket of them.

In 1989, an active debate was conducted in the UK as to whether or not Britain should join the Exchange Rate Mechanism. We had had one brief experience in the earlier version of the ERM, the snake, under Sir Edward Heath as Prime Minister in the early 1970s. Our membership was short-lived.

The foreign exchange pressures built up very quickly on sterling and it was soon thrown out of the system.

By 1989, much informed opinion in the country favoured entering the Exchange Rate Mechanism. I remember it well. The Confederation of British Industry, the Labour Party, leading members of the Conservative Cabinet, many commentators, economists and journalists all strongly supported going into the Exchange Rate Mechanism. They argued that we should be able to keep our currency stable against the Deutschmark, and that by doing so we would mirror Germany's performance in creating a low-inflation economy. Many felt that it would create greater stability. They pointed to the erratic inflation rates experienced in the UK in the post-war period compared with the lower and more stable inflation rate of Germany, and concluded that Britain would be better advised to steer her monetary policy by the Deutschmark than by her own domestic decisions.

Just before I joined the government in 1989, I wrote a pamphlet on Europe which set out the case against joining the Exchange Rate Mechanism. I was worried that our monetary policy was being debauched by shadowing the Deutschmark. Although we had not formally entered the Exchange Rate Mechanism, the Treasury had decided that keeping the pound relatively stable against the Deutschmark was the way to keep inflation down. They had fallen out of love with the Medium Term Financial Strategy setting targets for spending, taxing and borrowing and keeping under control the amount of money in circulation. These tools had been successful in the early to mid

73

1980s in keeping price rises under control. Their switch of policy proved to be a disaster.

The academic commentators in favour of the Exchange Rate Mechanism conceded that stability for Continental currencies had been made easier by capital and exchange controls limiting the free movement of monies. The abolition of these capital controls as part of the 1992 single market programme made Exchange Rate Mechanism control over exchange rates more difficult rather than easier. They also argued that because sterling was such a widely traded international currency it would be more difficult, to keep within the narrow bands than smaller less well traded currencies such as the florin or the Belgian franc.

I argued that the Exchange Rate Mechanism was likely to destabilise rather than stabilise the British economy. It meant the government was often forced into doing the opposite of what made sense for Britain. If people find the pound particularly attractive compared with the Deutschmark, they buy it and push up its value. In the ERM, all the central banks try to stop the pound going up and the mark going down by doing the oppsosite. They all sell pounds and buy Deutschmarks in an effort to counter the substantial commercial forces ranged on the other side. This action is destabilising. If the Bank of England sells a large amount of sterling in order to buy Deutschmarks, it then has a monetary problem. If it simply creates the pounds it has sold, it adds directly to the money supply. Foreign banks and other buyers then have more pounds at their disposal. If they go into the banking system, the money can be used by the banks to lend many times the original sum to customers. The banks have to keep only a small proportion of money in cash to pay depositors who want their money back, so they can lend on much more than is originally deposited, creating more credit. As a result, the amount of sterling in circulation rises.

Too much money then chases too few goods, causing increases in prices. The inflation that results encourages the central bank to raise interest rates to try to reduce the amount of borrowing. Once there has been a further increase in interest rates, sterling then looks even more attractive from the point of view of the overseas purchaser, leading to a further demand for pounds. More pounds are manufactured and sold by the Bank of England! These sums then find their way into the banking system, which uses them to multiply credit further. The ERM created a vicious circle which did grave damage to the economy.

The origins of the great inflation in Britain in the early 1990s lie in the attempts to shadow the Deutschmark in the later 1980s. Because at that point sterling was an attractive currency and wanted to up against the Deutschmark efforts to keep it down the money supply in the UK ballooned in the way I described. A credit explosion occurred in the late 1980s with billions of pounds of extra money being made available by the banks to lenders as a direct result of the extra money, created through the perverse consequences of the monetary policy that was followed in the name of stabilising the exchange rate, finding its way into the banking system.

The central bank does have some means of trying to offset this monetary problem. It puts itself into the ridiculous position of selling large quantities of gilt-edged securities to the private sector in order to counteract the monetary expansion caused by the foreign-exchange sales. If it sells long-term debt to the private sector, the buyers withdraw the money from the credit creating banks to purchase the debt securities, reducing the amount of money and therefore the amount of credit in the banking system. In the year to March 1988, the UK government collected £3,600 million more in taxes than it spent on public goods and services, but it none the less had to borrow an additional £7,000 million through the gilt-edged market in order to counterbalance the short-term monetary consequences of trying to shadow the Deutschmark. This has burdened British tax-payers for over twenty years with an additional £700 million a year of interest charges.

If the British authorities had not shadowed the Deutschmark, interest rates and even the exchange rate might have been more stable. Let us assume that, in the quarter to March 1988, the government had bought no Deutschmark or yen and sold no pounds. Instead of needing to borrow to counteract the monetary effects of issuing more pounds, the government could have repaid debt, further strengthening its strong financial position and cutting the interest burden in subsequent years. As a result of issuing less new debt and having better monetary control, interest rates would have remained at a lower level. In consequence, the pound would have been slightly less attractive to overseas buyers and might, therefore, have risen less fast and less far than it did under the interventionist scheme.

Unfortunately, the damage was done. The credit explosion occurred, in no small measure because Britain was selling pounds and creating pounds in an attempt to keep the value of the pound down. This in turn triggered an inflation which then needed drastic monetary action to correct. Broad money, a measure of how much more cash and credit was circulating in the economy, was growing by 15 or 16 per cent a year. While the financial statement in the Budget report proudly concluded that "sterling has shown considerable stability against the Deutschmark over the past year", it had to skate over the fact that money and credit had grown nearly 16 per cent in twelve months. Despite this huge increase in credit, the Treasury concluded that inflation would remain under good control. It was concentrating on the stability of the exchange rate rather than looking at what really mattered. In practice there was too much money chasing too few goods, so inflation was bound to surge.

A year later, in March 1989, the financial statement and Budget report had to note a further increase in money and credit growth to 17 per cent. Inflation had soared to 6 per cent by the fourth quarter of 1988, but the Treasury, looking at the exchange rate, was saying that inflation would fall decisively by the middle of 1990. The Treasury showed how far its policy had changed. It stated: "The exchange rate is a key influence, and a key indicator of, monetary conditions. It has to be considered together with all the evidence of domestic indicators in making monetary policy decisions. Monetary policy has the overriding task of defeating inflation: the government is accordingly not prepared to accommodate increases and domestic costs by exchange rate depreciation. Sterling has risen slightly against the Deutschmark over the past year. The dollar has also risen against

77

the Deutschmark, though it has shown little change against the yen".

Gradually, almost imperceptibly, the Treasury moved away from the mid-80s position of controlling the growth of credit and broad money in the economy to targeting the exchange rate as its main means of guiding policy. As a result, it completely misjudged the likely move in inflation and undermined the stability, the British economy had experienced in the period from 1981 to 1986. Far from declining as they had hoped inflation soared to 10 per cent by the fourth quarter of 1990.

The Treasury went on to say in its March 1989 statement that "exchange rates are also important in international economic relations. The improved co-operation between the G7 countries, who share a common counter inflation objective, has been clearly beneficial to the international community." It was at this juncture in British policy that policy-makers were interested not only in international co-operation at the European level, through shadowing the Exchange Rate Mechanism but also in co-operation with the Japanese and American authorities in a kind of super Exchange Rate Mechanism including the yen and the dollar as well as the principal European currencies. They mesmerised each other into believing that greater currency stability would prevent inflation. Greater currency stability between countries all experiencing rising inflation does not curb inflation at all and can be very misleading.

Any student of the Exchange Rate Mechanism period in British economics and politics must understand that there was an important shift of policy in the later 1980s before we entered the Exchange Rate Mechanism properly. As the Treasury Guidance Notes and its actions make clear, Britain was trying to keep the pound at around three Deutchmarks throughout the later 1980s. As a result, because the pound wished to go up, far too many pounds were printed and sold across the exchanges. It argued that if sterling was strong, there could be no recurrence of inflation. The damage was done and inflation soared from the acceptable levels of the mid-80s to double figures by the early 1990s. Had the original Medium Term Financial Strategy with a broad money target been continued in the later 1980s none of this would have happened.

It was on 8 October 1990 that the UK decided to join the Exchange Rate Mechanism formally. Having tried to keep the pound down to around 2.95 Deutschmarks – its chosen central rate in the ERM in the later 1980s, this was the chosen rate for entering the Exchange Rate Mechanism in October 1990. In practice, we had belonged to it already for many months. Sterling was someway off the peak it had reached of almost 3.3 Deutschmarks during the period of intense pressure in the late 1980s. The government patiently waited for it to come back to what it thought was a sensible, sustainable rate. It was an average rate that the pound had sustained over quite a long period, from the middle of 1986 onwards. Indeed, it was the rate that the government had clearly been trying to sustain during those years of proxy membership of the Exchange Rate Mechanism.

The Treasury explained the impact of the Exchange Rate Mechanism in its 1991/92 Financial Statement and Budget Report. "Interest rates remain the essential instrument of monetary policy, but now the overriding factor in setting them is the need to meet the UK's Exchange Rate Mechanism obligations." This was only a matter of degree, as monetary policy in the two or three years prior to entry had clearly been primarily determined by the wish to keep sterling in line with the Deutschmark. Now it was an open public commitment, however, the pressure intensified on the policy-makers to make it work. Any failure would entail a major loss of face. They could no longer tolerate the deviations that they had experienced in the shadow ERM period, and the speculators now knew for sure the narrow limits the currency was allowed. It gave them a great target to shoot at.

The Treasury went on to explain that "any loss of discretion to respond to domestic monetary conditions is likely to be more than compensated for by the improved market confidence and reduced inflationary expectations that the ERM commitment is bringing about". Britain decided to join the wider bands of the Exchange Rate Mechanism. Members of the wider bands could allow their currencies to move by plus or minus 6 per cent around their central rate. Those currencies in the narrow bands were permitted only a 2½ percentage point deviation either side of their central rate. By the time sterling entered the ERM formally, the pressures were more likely to be downwards than upwards. As a result of the proxy ERM period of monetary policy, Britain had experienced soaring inflation and had then had to raise interest rates dramatically to try to curb the credit boom. Just before entering the Exchange Rate Mechanism, interest rates were at 15 per cent. As part of the deal, Margaret

Thatcher insisted on a 1 percentage point drop in short-term interest rates in return for joining the Exchange Rate Mechanism. Britain therefore entered and posted short-term interest rates at 14 per cent. The die was now cast for a nasty recession, because once in the ERM, it was impossible to cut interest rates as far and as fast as was needed.

The case of those who favoured entry into the Exchange Rate Mechanism was positive, glowing and encouraging. They said that entering the Exchange Rate Mechanism would enable us to enjoy a "golden scenario". The golden scenario would mean that interest rates could come down, economic growth could be resumed and inflation would fall to low levels where it would remain. They had every confidence that the British economy could be brought into line with the German economy, and that the German economy would remain an anchor economy combining good growth with low inflation.

Some of us could never see how this was going to work. The German and British economies were at different stages of the cycle. The British economy was going into recession while the German economy was still expanding. Added to this was the complication that German reunification brought about. At exactly the point when Britain decided to link her fortunes irrevocably and publicly to the Deutschmark, the German authorities decided to debauch the Deutschmark by going in for a hasty and generous currency union with East Germany. It did not matter that the German central bank argued against this move. It did not matter that informed commentators around the world said that a currency union of the two Germanies on generous terms to the East Germans would be inflationary. It meant printing a huge number of new DM to give to people in eastern Germany in return for their less valuable Ost marks. Too much money was chasing too few goods, so prices were bound to soar.

None the less the exponents of the "golden scenario" held to their ground. With considerable difficulty, the government managed to edge interest rates down during our period in the Exchange Rate Mechanism, although they remained well above the levels that British industry and commerce could live with as the recession intensified. In March 1992, the Treasury explained that membership of the Exchange Rate Mechanism was to meet the convergence criteria of the Maastricht treaty. "ERM member-ship will remain the central discipline underpinning UK macro-economic policy in a medium term." The Treasury was confident that with a little more pain and a little more pressure, and a bit longer taking the nasty medicine of high interest rates, the period of adjustment would be over.

The Treasury briefed ministers to tell people that the recession would be relatively shallow and short-lived, and that recovery would follow quite rapidly after the general election in the spring of 1992. The public was extremely sceptical about this. By now, a long period of high interest rates, needed to correct the credit explosion of the late 1980s, was bankrupting businesses, driving house prices down and doing all sorts of economic damage. None the less the Treasury looked to the future and stated: "Sterling will move to narrow bounds within the Exchange Rate Mechanism in due course, maintaining its central rate at 2.95 Deutschmarks."

With the general election out of the way and the Conservative government duly re-elected, the recession intensified. Instead of the predictions coming true that recovery would follow as night follows day, the British economy struggled to deal with the very high interest rates needed to maintain sterling's position in the Exchange Rate Mechanism. By the autumn of 1992, speculators began to decide that the pain inflicted on the British economy was too great and that sterling would have to leave the Exchange Rate Mechanism.

The government was reluctant to accept defeat. It threw every-thing into the battle. Millions of pounds of foreign exchange reserves were sold across the exchanges in order to buy up pounds in the hope that this would bolster the value of sterling. It was decided that interest rates had to be increased. On the final day in the Exchange Rate Mechanism, interest rates were hoisted back up to 12 per cent and a beleaguered Chancellor of the Exchequer said that they would return to 15 per cent the following morning. It was a sign that he was prepared to try anything to demonstrate the government's commitment to the Exchange Rate Mechanism, to appease the markets, to persuade them that the pound would be defended.

Unfortunately, it was all to no avail. The market forces were simply too great. Spending foreign exchange reserves on buying up pounds did the opposite of what was needed to the UK economy in the recession. Every hundred million pounds bought up removed credit from the system. At a time when businesses were desperate for more bank lending to keep them going through very difficult trading conditions, banks instead had to call in their loans and cut the credit in the system in response to the purchase and destruction of pounds through foreign exchange intervention. The country had to borrow billions of pounds of convertible foreign currencies in order to sell them across the exchanges to buy up sterling. As a result, the tax-payer was lumbered with further debts in the name of stabilisation policy. Despite billions of pounds of foreign exchange intervention, despite the two increases in interest rates, despite clear strong government commitment to the Exchange Rate Mechanism, on 16 September 1992 it was decided to give in and accept that market forces were too strong. The speculators had exploited the weaknesses of the system to make themselves a fortune. The taxpayer was left nursing his collective losses, and the British economy was deeply damaged by the whole experience.

The damage done was very considerable. The years 1991 and 1992 saw falls in national income and output. Unemployment soared to three million. Thousands of businesses went bankrupt. There was endless bad news about redundancies, closed companies and struggling enterprises. It was a policy urged on the government by the opposition parties and the CBI. They never said we should leave the ERM. The government carried the can and had to shoulder the blame, yet it was a big mistake of the whole British political and commercial establishment. There were not many of us who had warned in advance that it could not work.

The British economy needed much lower interest rates, some credit growth, a substantial easing of the pain. This came quite rapidly once we had removed ourselves from the Exchange Rate

Mechanism. By March 1993, the Treasury could report short-term interest rates down to 6 per cent, the lowest rates in the European Community. The long-term interest rates had fallen 1 point from the February 1992 level. Monetary policy had changed again, for the better.

The Treasury stated: "last autumn, following the suspension of sterling's membership of the Exchange Rate Mechanism, the government put in place a new policy framework for its counter-inflation strategy." While it is a little ominous that the Treasury talks only about the suspension of sterling's membership of the Exchange Rate Mechanism, probing questions in the House of Commons persuaded the Prime Minister to confirm that the government had no intention of re-entering the Exchange Rate Mechanism in the lifetime of the 1992 to 1997 Parliament. As a result, the government needed a new economic policy framework. The Treasury went on to state: "while the pound remains outside the Exchange Rate Mechanism, decisions about interest rates are based on a continuing assessment of monetary conditions, measured principally by the growth of narrow and broad money, and movements in the exchange rate and asset prices."

This was a very sensible new policy. The idea that broad money, a way of looking at credit expansion generally in the economy, did matter and should have an impact on monetary policy brought the system back to some common sense. What the Treasury had known in the mid-80s and had deliberately forgotten in the later 1980s and early 1990s in its pursuit of currency stability against the DM was reintroduced to an important place in policy-making. As a result, it was possible to set interest rates that made sense for British industry and commerce.

The plunging interest rates and the modest increase in credit eased the pressures on the business community dramatically. Unemployment started to fall month by month. Slowly and gradually business confidence started to rebuild and the economy started to grow again. The Treasury feared that inflation would pick up because of the devaluation, but the subsequent couple of years demonstrated that this was a totally ungrounded fear. Inflation was not going to pick up then, because credit had been very strongly controlled during our period in the Exchange Rate Mechanism and could continue to be controlled all the time the government followed a sensible monetary policy.

By November 1994, the Treasury could state: "sterling has remained stable against a basket of currencies this year, although it has appreciated against the dollar and depreciated against the main European currencies and the yen." Of course, immediately on leaving the Exchange Rate Mechanism there was a sharp downward movement in sterling against the Deutschmark and Deutschmark-related currencies. Several other European currencies also succumbed to the same pressures at the same time. The escudo, the lira, the peseta, the Finnish markka and the Swedish krona all devalued. It was not a sterling crisis. It was more a Deutschmark crisis with the Deutschmark wishing to go up and the other currencies taking the strain. The German central bank put everything into the defence of the franc, but was not so willing to defend the other currencies of the system.

On leaving the Exchange Rate Mechanism Britain, was able to follow a policy geared to the interests of the domestic and exporting economy. One of the big problems during the period in the Exchange Rate Mechanism was the discovery that the Deutschmark might drag the pound to a value against the dollar which did not suit Britain's trade. Britain has a large trade in dollar-denominated products. For example, Aerospace products, computer products and other hi-tech industrial goods are commonly priced in dollars. As a leading exporter in these industries and a leading location for American companies based in Europe, Britain needed a competitive pound against the dollar in order to carry on trading successfully in these industries. During the period of Deutschmark strength in 1991–2, the pound was dragged to unrealistic levels against the dollar, doing considerable damage to the exports and the industrial capability of these important industries.

It also hit our tourism. American tourists often prefer to come to London and the UK rather than Continental centres when visiting Europe. The common language, history and culture are the principle attractions. None the less, if the pound becomes too overvalued against the dollar, the attraction can prove too expensive. By the middle of 1992, there was a notable shortage of American tourists in London.

We also learnt in our Exchange Rate Mechanism period that the forces of speculators are considerably greater than the money and power available even to central banks and governments working in concert. The volumes of money traded across the

87

exchanges every day vastly exceed the reserves of even the richest countries. If the marketplaces decide that a currency is too high or too low, there is little that the concerted intervention of central banks can do about it. Even a government prepared to raise interest rates to totally unacceptable levels in the middle of a recession, and to borrow billions of pounds to sure up its currency position was unable to defend its currency against speculative pressures.

Third, let's hope we have learnt that the Exchange Rate Mechanism is destabilising. Even the present government, keen to join the euro and to bring the British economy into line with the German and French economies, is shy about re-entering. Unfortunately, joining the Exchange Rate Mechanism does not offer a sure-fire way of guaranteeing low inflation or stable policy.

What relevance does the Exchange Rate Mechanism experience have to those considering joining a single currency? It should be seen as central evidence in the case. Proponents of the single currency are in effect recycling the old golden scenario that ERM exponents produced in the late 1980s. What is surprising is that they are prepared to try again when the experience with the ERM was so bitter. The exponents of the single currency say that it will remove currency fluctuations. They say that it will lower inflationary expectations and it will build business confidence. They believe that because the currency area is bigger somehow that makes it better and more stable.

On the contrary, what they should worry about is that joining a single currency is like rejoining the Exchange Rate Mechanism but this time throwing away the key to the locked door. Imagine what would have happened in September 1992 if we had not been able to get out of the Exchange Rate Mechanism. Interest rates would have gone up further to defend the ECU. The recessionary forces in the economy would have been intensified. Far from unemployment coming down and business confidence growing the reverse would have happened.

The exponents of the single currency say that the absence of George Soros and the speculative hordes working away against sterling, had we joined the single currency, would mean that belonging to the euro would be completely different. They miss the fundamental point. If you give away the power to allow the exchange rate to take the strain, the strain of adjustment would inevitably fall on the real economy. Instead of the sterling rate changing, factories close, people lose their jobs, the adjustment process is much more painful.

Nor is it possible to divorce belonging to the Exchange Rate Mechanism from the single currency. It is a condition to joining the single currency that a country has led a stable life in the Exchange Rate Mechanism for two years prior to entry. The Community has always stuck to its view that the best way to a single currency is to demonstrate ever-growing convergence of the currencies that wish to join by seeing them in an association called the Exchange Rate Mechanism.

The Dublin Summit reconfirmed this by establishing the second Exchange Rate Mechanism. This, we are told, is a different mechanism from the one it replaces. Rather than being based on cross-rates from one currency to the others, it is based on a hub-

89

and-spoke principle, tied to a central rate to the Euro. This is playing with words. If each currency has a fixed exchange rate to the central currency in the system, then you can also work out the cross-rates between all the currencies in the system. Similarly, in the old ERM, had you nominated a currency or the ECU as the anchor of the system, it would have been possible to work out the rate to that. The essential characteristics of the two Exchange Rate Mechanisms are the same. They are based upon the proposition that the participating currencies must stay within narrow bands of each other. They are based on the proposition that central banks must make their prime aim of policy the establishment of stable currencies against the other member currencies. They assume that the combined powers of the central banks and governments will outstrip the combined powers of the speculators, and they assume that the economies and currencies are sufficiently converged to be able to live happily together. So far, speculators have left the euro system alone. They believe that the twelve countries in the new ERM do plan to merge and adopt the euro in 2002, so they accept the rates of exchange the politicians have established. They might not take such a relaxed view if sterling went back in as part of a programme to try to bring the UK into line with Euroland. The UK economy is a large one, and will not behave in the same way as the core of Euroland.

Between 1983 and 1987, UK real national income rose by 14 per cent. Price inflation had been at or below 5 per cent and Sterling had stayed on average at around $1.50 to the pound. It is true there had been currency fluctuations, but the general performance of the economy was stable. There was good average growth year on year, unemployment was coming down and inflation was under reasonable control. Between 1987 and 1993, we had a period of intense turbulence. Growth shot up, inflation shot up, the economy was then plunged into a deep recession. Inflation shot down, unemployment rose dramatically and a lot of damage was done to British business. The first period is the period of the Medium Term Financial Strategy driven by control of broad and narrow money and a pragmatic approach to running the economy. The second period is the period of ideological commitment to the sterling/Deutschmark rate. The results of the experiment are very clear for all to see. The Exchange Rate Mechanism was destabilising, the pragmatic Medium Term Financial Strategy was friendly to growth and development of the economy. Since 1992, we have returned to most of the virtues of a pragmatic Medium Term Financial Strategy. As a result we have seen another era of good growth, low inflation and falling unemployment.

Advocates of the single currency say that the absence of speculative pressures makes all the difference. They are right in one respect. If we abolished the pound, then the British government could not be driven into extreme measures to defend the pound's value. However, if we were in a single currency it would, in many other respects, be the same as being in the Exchange Rate Mechanism but without the right to get out. Monetary policy would be set in the general interests of the union as a whole. If the union is not a reasonable homogenous area with common economic activity, then the interest rate set overall might be too lax or too severe for the British part of the union. Britain would feel what some in Scotland felt in 1988/9. Some Scots felt that the Scottish economy was not booming like the English economy, yet Scotland had to experience the higher interest rates needed to correct the monetary excesses for the UK as a whole. This could often be the position Britain faced in a currency union with our Continental partners. It is the position Ireland faces today inside the euro area, with interest rates that are far too low for her own economy, resulting in accelerating inflation.

Advocates of currency union say that this means Britain wishes to keep open the devaluation option. That is not my position at all. I want to keep open the option of making the adjustment, whether it be upwards or downwards, through the currency rather than through some more direct and painful means. Given the pattern of Britain's trade, it is not only the Deutschmark rate that matters to us. Getting the wrong value of our currency against the dollar can be even more damaging. In the late 1980s I did not wish us to pursue the devaluation option: I wished us to pursue the revaluation option. Had in the late 1980s allowed sterling to rise more rapidly than we did, we could have avoided some of the excesses and problems we experienced. Conversely, when the Deutschmark was too strong in 1992, it would have been better to have allowed the pound to devalue against the Deutschmark yet keep a sensible value against the dollar.

Many who favour European integration look back on the Exchange Rate Mechanism experience and say that the failing was the initial rate at which we entered. At least they do not argue that the British government failed to put in the effort necessary to try and make it work. Everyone in the debate concedes that the British Government tried everything in its power in August and September 1992 to try and save the pound. No one suggests we should have squandered or borrowed even more billions in an effort to sustain an unsustainable sterling.

The argument that 2.95 Deutschmarks to the pound was the wrong rate is a very curious one. It was not an argument made by the advocates of the Exchange Rate Mechanism when we entered. I would have more sympathy with the advocates had they made this clear at the time. When we entered, people commented on how wise the government had been in waiting for sterling to come back about 10 per cent from its high against the Deutschmark over the previous year before fixing the rate. Commentators felt that it was a sensible rate at which to enter and it was based on the average rate that we had experienced for many months before making the decision to go public. As we have seen, it was related to the rate the Treasury had been using for many months in its efforts to shadow the German currency.

It is true that the advocates of entry knew that, in order to make it work, there had to be a change in price and wage behaviour by British businesses. They made that very clear to British businesses, and many businesses tried to respond. What were the other options available to the British government? Given that they wanted to enter the Exchange Rate Mechanism then, there were not many. They could have chosen a rate five or ten pfennigs lower than the one they chose. Given that the pound fell 15 per cent against the Deutschmark in September 1992 on exit from the ERM, 5 or 10 pfennigs either way would probably have not made very much difference to the eventual outcome. Had the government tried to devalue the pound on entry into the Exchange Rate Mechanism, one of two things would have happened. People might have taken the devaluation as a strong signal that the British government was not serious about the discipline of the Exchange Rate Mechanism. Alternatively, the markets might not have believed the devaluation and would have immediately placed sterling under upward pressure. Neither of these proposals rightly recommended themselves to the government at the time.

The problem with this thought process is in the assumption. There is no right rate for sterling against the Deutschmark which you can fix and hold in perpetuity. The long history of sterling against the Deutschmark, the dollar, the yen and any other major world currency is one of fluctuations and trend movements. It so happens that in the post-war period sterling has been in a down trend against the Deutschmark. Similarly, in the inter-war period Sterling was in a pronounced up trend against the then German currency which was a by-word for financial irresponsibility.

There is a right rate today for Sterling against the Deutschmark and there will be a right rate in three months' time but it will be a remarkable coincidence if these two correct rates are the same. The purpose of the exchange rate is to allow people to freely exchange German currency for British currency, or vice versa. It is a market like any other, and the price adjusts according to the balance of buyers and sellers. They take into account their views on how well or badly the British and German economies are performing and whether or not the British and German monetary authorities are equally serious about maintaining the value of their money and curbing inflation. The best way for the British authorities to keep the value of the pound high against the euro/DM if that is their main aim, is to pursue tight control of credit and inflation at home, so that people gain confidence in the currency. You do not have to belong to the Exchange Rate Mechanism to do this: indeed experience in the late 1980's shows that it can be damaging to base your policy on shadowing another currency.

Those who would like us to join the single currency must be contemplating our re-entry into the Exchange Rate Mechanism in order to qualify. Should we go back in at today's rate of 3.15 DM, or should we wait to see if the pound will fall back to 2.70 or even 2.50 DM? To pose such a question should show anyone the foolishness of the idea that there is a right rate. If we choose too low a rate, we will have inflation; and if choose too high a rate we will have factory closures. The government has refused to be drawn into any discussion of how you would determine the right rate for entry, or how you would persuade our partners to accept a different rate from the 2.95 DM rate which remains our central rate for the Exchange Rate Mechanism. The British Liberal Democrat party, keen to enter the euro as soon as possible, established a high-level working party to look into this matter. They concluded it was a very important and difficult question, and that a substantial devaluation would be needed before entry. They have not explained how this would be engineered in the markets, or why our partners should accept it.

If you follow a policy based on taking a clear view of how much credit there should be in your own economy and what inflation rate you wish to create in your own economy, then you have a chance of success. If you gear your policy to shadowing another country's currency, then your own domestic economy is subject to the vagaries and random events that other countries, policies can create for you. It was not Britain's choice that Chancellor Kohl decided to debauch the Deutschmark in the early 1990s by the currency union of the two Germanies, but that became a most important policy which had a big impact on Britain. As Germany sucked in more and more credit and more and more money to fuel the rebuilding of eastern Germany, so more and more pressure was placed on the pound.

Searching for the right rate of the pound against the euro is like searching for the Holy Grail. It would be great if you could discover it, but experience teaches us that it will never be found.

Ten problems with rigged exchange rates

1 In the late 1980s, we kept the pound down, tying it to the DM. That gave us a bad dose of inflation, as it meant interest rates were too low and too much money was printed.

2 In the early 1990s, we kept the pound up – tying it to the DM in the Exchange Rate Mechanism. Interest rates were kept too high to defend the pound, there was a tight credit squeeze, and a deep recession.

3 If we had joined the euro on day one, the pound would now be much lower against the dollar, making it much dearer to buy all the things we do from the USA.

4 The euro does not give you exchange rate stability – it gives

businessmen bigger headaches with the dollar and the yen, as these go up and down more against the euro than against the pound.

5   There is no right rate for the pound against the DM or the euro that will work for all time. Many said 2.95DM was the right rate in 1989, only to say in 1992 that it was obviously the wrong rate.

6   If you cannot devalue your currency when your costs are too high, you have to sack people and close factories instead.

7   If you cannot revalue your currency when your economy is going well, you have to raise taxes to stop overheating instead.

8   Businessmen say they want currency stability, but they do not want the wrong interest rates, high inflation, or recession that often goes with keeping a currency stable against a different currency and economy.

9   You cannot make currencies behave the same unless you first bring the two economies into line.

10 History shows that rigged exchange rates do not work. The Gold Standard, pegging currencies such as the pound to the price of gold, bankrupted many businesses and caused mass unemployment. The snake in the 1970s failed to keep the pound at a constant value against the Continental currencies. The Exchange Rate Mechanism caused a bad recession, and then collapsed.

Chapter five

Why a single economic policy will not work

Following the Maastricht Treaty, the euro members have pressed on with creating a common economic policy. Under Article 102a: "Member states shall conduct their economic policies with a view to contributing to the achievement of the objectives of the Community, as defined in Article 2, and in the context of the broad guidelines referred to in Article 103(2)." Article 2 is an Article of principle, stating that economic union is an aim, requiring "a harmonious and balanced development of economic activities, sustainable and non-inflationary growth respecting the environment, a high degree of convergence of economic performance, a high level of employment and of social protection, the raising of the standard of living and the quality of life, and economic and social cohesion and solidarity among member states".

Each member state has a duty to co-ordinate its economic policies with the others. The Council, on a recommendation from the Commission, is charged with the task of agreeing broad guidelines for the economic polices of the member states. Member states have to supply regular information about their economic policies and performance to the Commission, who report on it to the Council. If a member state is thought to be following a policy outside the European guidelines, or generally unhelpful to economic and monetary union, the Council decides the policy is inconsistent and may make its conclusions public.

This approach is buttressed by stronger measures in specific economic areas. The original EEC treaties established a customs union, with a common external tariff, and the abolition of most customs duties and quantitative restrictions on trade between member states. It established a common agricultural policy, whose aims included the stabilisation of markets and the creation of one market controlling organisation. It included a common fisheries policy, the free movement of persons, capital and services, the beginnings of a common transport policy and common competition and commercial policies.

The Maastricht Treaty takes the creation of a common economic policy a lot further than the predecessor treaties. The deliberate establishment of a Community monetary policy and a single currency in effect create a single economic policy, by having one exchange rate, one interest rate and one set of rules over borrowing for all member states. Once the euro is fully established, it will be impossible for countries to follow widely divergent policies, because they will no longer control the main levers of economic policy. The Treaty of Nice strengthens the grip over industrial and trade policy.

The main test of convergence for economic policies is laid out in the Protocol to the Maastricht Treaty. Controlling budget deficits is central to this task.

How states would lose control of their budgets

Monetary union entails passing substantial control over economic policy to European institutions. Supporters of the single currency imply that it is a technical matter: yet it is a fundamental matter, which goes to the heart of what government can do.

Member states are instructed to avoid excessive government deficits. If different member states persevered with differing levels of deficits under a common currency scheme, the high borrowing state, would take advantage of the lower-borrowing member states.

The rate of interest a government borrows at is related to the amount you need to borrow and to the likely future value of your currency. In a single currency area, currency variability has been removed, and all borrow at a similar interest rate. Before the introduction of the euro, with fourteen different national currencies, each state borrowed at a different interest rate based on the market's view of its credit-worthiness, the amount it wanted to borrow and the likely strength of its currency. In the single currency scheme, if member states could carry on borrowing as much as they liked, the high-borrowing countries would help drive up the average rate of interest that the lower-borrowing country had to borrow at, because the markets would look at the credit-worthiness and quantity of borrowing of the governments as a whole, being unable to set different interest rates for each currency. They might differentiate between the credit-worthiness of the various governments, but the variation would be small.

Naturally, the EU feels that there must be some limit on the profligate to protect the prudent, and to keep EU interest rates down to sensible levels. The treaty sets out an elaborate procedure to do just this. It states:

The Commission shall monitor the development of the budgetary situation and of the stock of government debt in the member states with a view to identifying gross errors. In particular it shall examine compliance with budgetary discipline on the basis of the following two criteria:

a) whether the ratio of the planned or actual government deficit to gross domestic product exceeds a reference value, unless either the ratio has declined substantially and continuously and reached a level that comes close to the reference value; or, alternatively, the excess over the reference value is only exceptional and temporary and the ratio remains close to the reference value;

b) whether the ratio of government debt to gross domestic product exceeds a reference value, unless the ratio is sufficiently diminishing and approaching the reference value at a satisfactory pace.

These requirements are better defined in the Protocol attached to the treaty on excessive deficits. These specify that the annual government deficit should not be more than 3 per cent of gross domestic product (GDP), and that the stock of government debt should not exceed 60 per cent of GDP.

Government debt as a percentage of GDP, end 2000

Austria	64%	
Belgium	111%	
Denmark	48%	(non euro member)
Finland	44%	*cont'd* . . .

France	59%	
Germany	60%	
Greece	103%	
Ireland	37%	
Italy	111%	
Netherlands	58%	
Portugal	56%	
Spain	61%	
Sweden	58%	(non euro member)
UK	43%	(non euro member)

When the decision was made to allow most of the countries into the euro scheme, the EU *de facto* relaxed these requirements. Even France and Germany struggled to reduce their budget deficits to 3 per cent. Countries took obligations off the balance sheet, or received money in return for accepting longer-term obligations, to lower the deficit in the qualifying years. For example, the French raised money by accepting obligations to pay Telecom pensions in future years. Since countries joined the scheme, strong action has been taken to keep budget deficits below 3 per cent, although several countries, including Italy, Belgium and Greece, are still well above the 60 per cent ceiling for total debt. The EU Council decided to ignore this require-ment as too few countries could get anywhere near meeting it. It reminds us all that this is a political scheme driven by political imperatives. It is not a technical bankers' scheme driven by ratios, figures and economic requirements.

If a member state does have an excessive deficit or is likely to run one, the Commission, under the treaty, has to take action.

The Commission prepares a report which it presents to the Monetary Committee established under the treaty. The Committee gives an opinion on the Commission finding, which is then put to the Council of Ministers. The Council ultimately decides if the Commission is correct, voting by qualified, or weighted, majority on whether there is or is not an excessive deficit. If there is, the Council makes proposals to the member state to correct the deficit.

If the member state fails to sort things out following this action, the Council can then publish its findings and recommendations, in the hope that public pressure will force the necessary adjustments. If the member state still fails to do so, the Council can instruct it to do so, and demand reports on how it is getting on. If the member state is still delinquent, the Council can invite the European Investment Bank to reconsider its lending policy towards the member state concerned; it can require a non-interest bearing deposit to be lodged, or it can impose fines.

These are draconian powers. If properly enforced, it means that member states would be unable to borrow more than 3 per cent of their GDP in any year, and would be unable to make any new borrowings at all if they have reached an outstanding stock of debt equal to 60 per cent of their GDP. All this would be enforced by escalating from public shame to deposits and fines, sufficiently large to force the member state to act.

For any individual country, the flexibility that we see at work in practice might come to be an intrusion rather than welcome common sense. A government could not be sure in advance when it might trigger the excessive deficit procedure, given that several countries technically trigger it anyway because of their starting level of established debt. Further clarification of how much latitude is allowed and how it might be used would be most welcome, otherwise budgetary planning in most member states after joining the single currency will continue to be problematic.

So far, member states have wrestled with the need under the treaty to cut their budget deficits by a combination of tax increases and spending reductions. The British government, which decided on deficit reduction for a variety of reasons, relied in the early years on tax increases. Subsequently, growth has picked up following the exit from the ERM, allowing the deficit to reduce while spending rises. Other European countries have taken longer to get to grips with the problem. Most Continental countries have concentrated on spending cuts. The first big round of French spending cuts led to street protests and union opposition. Some of the proposals were amended as a result. In Germany's case, the cuts were very large. Spain also introduced large budget cuts.

Those who claim that enough budgetary control would remain in the hands of member states usually point to the fact that a member state could still raise both spending and taxation, or lower them, leaving the deficit unchanged. As we will see in chapter six, it is quite likely that a country setting out to pursue a policy of low taxation would be blocked. Such a country would anyway have to make a bigger contribution to the extra public spending which the single currency community will generate.

In the UK, some of the large unions have moved from Euro-enthusiasm to Euro-scepticism on the currency issue, as they now believe that huge budget cuts would be needed to qualify and stay in. They see this as a direct assault on the jobs and livelihoods of their members. For those of us who want a smaller state the prospect of this policy is still unappealing, as we see that the cuts would be clumsy, often damaging things that are needed, while government in total would grow as the European Union built up its own pattern of spending. I do not want Britain to have to sack nurses and teachers in order to pay the salaries of more officials in Brussels.

The Council of Ministers and the Commission will gradually seek more and more control over budgets and deposits. The Central Bank needs to know the totals and timings of member states borrowings in order to manage the markets. The budget rules of the treaty are already being extended by the Stability Pact.

Converging inflation rates

When the treaty was signed, the emphasis was on zero inflation. The wording of the treaty states that the European Central Bank has to achieve price stability. Since its establishment, the European Central Bank has chosen to ignore this, or interpret it as meaning low inflation, not no inflation. Low inflation is seen as an essential prerequisite, and rightly so. The shock of going into a single currency run for zero inflation would be crippling for an economy used to 5-10 per cent inflation. The tighter money policy would immediately reduce the credit available, closing factories and sacrificing jobs. The authors of the treaty stated that no country should have an inflation rate more than 1.5 per cent above the average of the best three. They assumed the best three performers would be experiencing inflation of around 1-2 per cent, so that the shock of going from that to 0 per cent would be containable. The results of this system so far has been to allow much faster inflation in the Euroland economies than in the three EU countries not part of the single currency. The peripheral economies in the Iberian peninsula, Greece and Ireland have pushed the average inflation rate much higher in Euroland. If the rate was calculated by adjusting for number of people in each country it would be lower in both Euroland and the three non-euro members.

Inflation in EU countries annual change, December 2000

Austria	1.8%
Belgium	3.0%
Denmark	2.3%
Finland	2.9%
France	1.7%
Germany	2.3%
Greece	3.7%
Ireland	4.6%
Italy	2.8%
Luxembourg	4.3%
Netherlands	2.9%
Portugal	3.8%
Spain	4.0%
Sweden	1.3%
UK	0.9%

cont'd . . .

| Euroland average | 3.15% |
| Non-euro EU members average | 1.5% |

The other requirement was the convergence of interest rates. Again, the Protocol is very clear. It says that a member state seeking to join has to show that its nominal average interest rates on long-term government bonds are not more than 2 per cent above the three lowest-inflation countries. Again, this is a sensible requirement, even a generous one. Once each country is in the currency union, its interest rates should snap into line. There would be little difference in perceived risk as between the German and French governments because under the rules, no country is able to borrow too much and get into repayment difficulties. The treaty aim is to make sure that on entry member states do not immediately receive a big bonus for other countries' hard work in reducing their long-term interest rates.

The treaty has another important clause referring to the exchange rate. Article 109(j) says that "The observance of the normal fluctuation margins provided for by the Exchange Rate Mechanism of the European Monetary System, for at least two years, without devaluing against the currency of any other member state" is also a requirement.

The Protocol reinforces this message:

The criterion . . . shall mean that a member state has respected the normal fluctuation margins provided for by the Exchange Rate Mechanism of the European Monetary System without severe tensions for at least two years before the examination. In particular, the member state shall not have devalued its currency's bilateral central rate against any other member's currency on its own initiative for the same period.

This too is a pre-eminently sensible requirement for countries contemplating the abolition of their own currencies. If a currency cannot stay in line with the others in the system, it means that the economies are not working happily together. Preventing adjustment through currency realignment by merging the currencies will mean the adjustments take place in more painful ways – by factory closures, bankrupt businesses and lost jobs. We saw this process at work in the last days of the ERM and its narrow bands, before the system fell apart.

The countries and currencies going forward to euro membership have more or less met this exchange rate requirement. Greece devalued within the ERM and served probation at the new rate before being admitted. Ireland was granted a small revaluation before locking rates for conversion. The UK government is reluctant to believe that ERM service is still necessary for membership of the Euro. Some favour the idea that a country like the UK could qualify if other member states agreed that the pound had been stable enough outside the ERM, on criteria still to be established. The problem with this approach is that it is not legal under the treaty, so any aggrieved person or company, if we proceed on this basis, could take the matter to court.

Many commentators are worried that the convergence criteria are all about monetary matters, and that none is about the real economy. It is possible for countries with totally different economies to qualify under these terms. For example, a country with half the income per head of the average could so order its monetary affairs to meet the requirements. Labour Party critics in Britain wished to see living standards, growth, employment and other crucial matters also taken into account. They were overruled by Continental plans.

Britain can, of course, apply such criteria herself to her own possible entry, given the flexible nature of the opt-out. The Chancellor has said that there are five economic tests which he will apply before deciding to recommend membership to the British people in a referendum. These tests go wider than the requirements of the treaty, but they are most imprecise. The British government refuses to tell us how the economic tests will be measured, over what time period, and what will constitute sufficient convergence for them to recommend going ahead. Indeed, the Treasury even blocks questions asking whether we are getting any nearer to meeting the five tests, or whether current policy is designed to let us pass the tests. The tests include the impact on the City of London and jobs, as well as the more traditional euro convergence questions.

The single economic policy of the treaty is incomplete. It is all about exchange rates, money and inflation. It ignores jobs, incomes and output. If pursued to its conclusion, it could easily alienate the voters of Europe, who think jobs and income are more important than financial matters. As the single currency is implemented, the participants will be asked to centralise and harmonise more and more of their economic policies. One currency, one bank, one interest rate will lead inevitably to common taxation, one budget and one economic policy, as the politicians of western Europe struggle with the unruly forces the euro unleashes, and as they go on their way of creating a country called Europe.

Slower growth in the single currency

The biggest argument put forward in favour of the single currency is that it would lead to faster growth. There are three main supporting points in this case. The first is the savings on foreign exchange transaction costs. The second is the lower nominal interest rates the low inflation forecast for the single currency would help bring about. The third is the lower real interest rate exponents of the scheme believe would follow as night follows day with its introduction.

In his book *In With the Euro, out With the Pound*, Christopher Johnson states that Britain which has been growing at 1.9 per cent a year since 1979, would, if it joined the single currency, have a chance to raise growth rates to a steady 2¾ to 3 per cent per annum. A 1 per cent increase in the growth rate would be a prize well worth considering, greatly adding to prosperity and employment prospects.

The idea that Britain's interest rate might fall if it were connected more strongly with the German economy is a curious one. Between 1980 and 1994, the long-term real interest rate that Britain was paying for its investment borrowing was a little lower than the German one and 0.8 per cent lower than the French one. When Britain was connected with the Exchange Rate Mechanism, it had long-term interest rates of between 9 and 12 per cent nominal. Since leaving the Exchange Rate Mechanism, long-term rates have been well below 8 per cent nominal. The pattern of short term rates has been even more dramatic. In the ERM period, rates were between 10 and 15 per cent. In the post

ERM period, they have been between 5½ and 6½ per cent. There is no evidence whatsoever that by joining a single currency Britain would automatically enjoy lower long-term interest rates than if it continues to conduct its own monetary policy. It is true that during the first two years of the euro scheme, short rates on the Continent have been lower than in the UK, but long-term rates for companies and mortgage rates have been a little lower in Britain than in Euroland. These two differences are not surprising. Euroland has needed lower short-term rates because its economy has been more sluggish than the UK's, while long-term borrowing rates have been lower in the UK because the UK government has been repaying debt. We would not have enjoyed the full advantage of this if we had joined the Euro, because then our long term rates would be dragged up by the higher borrowing countries.

Critics of British monetary policy since the war can rightly point to the fact that there have been times when risks have been taken with inflation, usually resulting in a period of higher interest rates than would otherwise have been needed or would have been desirable in order to choke off the inflation. Far from reducing the risk of this, shadowing the Deutschmark in the late 1980s and entering the Exchange Rate Mechanism in 1990 made this problem worse. Conversely, the periods between 1981 and between 1987 and 1992 and the present day demonstrate that Britain is capable of conducting a sensible monetary policy, and when she does so she can enjoy relatively low interest rates.

Whichever way you look at the figures of growth, you have to conclude that the problem that Europe faces is one of a lack of competitiveness inducing slow growth rates throughout the European Community area. Between 1991 and 1996, the OECD economies, the main free enterprise economies of the world, grew by 10 per cent. The fifteen countries of the European Community grew only 7.6 per cent in those five years, yet the UK grew by 10.8 per cent. More recently, the Euroland economies have been catching up, and the UK has become more sluggish, thanks to higher taxes, higher regulatory costs and higher interest rates imposed by the Labour government. They seem keen to bring the UK economy into line by lowering its growth rate. The best way of doing this is to adopt Euroland levels of taxation and regulation which make economies less competitive and slow them down. And even though the US has been growing faster for many more years, US growth is still ahead of Euroland growth:

Growth Rates of GDP, third quarter 2000 annual change %

Austria	3.9%
Belgium	4.5%
Denmark	3.6%
Finland	4.5%
France	3.1%
Germany	3.4%
Greece	3.4%
Ireland	9.8%
Italy	2.4%
Luxembourg	7.5%
Netherlands	3.6%
Portugal	3.7%
Spain	3.9%

cont'd . . .

Sweden	4.0%
UK	2.9%
USA	5.3%

More recently the US economy has slowed down markedly, but so too has the German Economy.

Christopher Johnson himself in his book illustrates that Britain's annual average growth rate of 1.9 per cent between 1980 and 1994 is almost bang in line with the European Community's 2 per cent per annum and is identical to the French and Italian growth rates over that fourteen-year period. These growth rates are below that in the United States of America which came out at 2.3 per cent and well below the stunningly good growth rates of Asian countries such as China, Singapore and Hong Kong. By taking the period from 1980 to 1994, British experience is put in the worst possible light, as it includes two major recessions – one at either end of the chosen period. Carrying the figures through to 2000 would produce a more favourable comparison for the UK.

The proponents of the single currency scheme are quite right in saying that if the scheme were implemented and made controlling inflation its prime task, it would create an area of lower nominal interest rates. Germany in the post-war period has enjoyed lower nominal interest rates than Britain or Italy or France, because she has been a lower-inflation economy. Britain could achieve the same herself by pursuing tight monetary policies that regard the control of inflation as the prime or only function of monetary policy. The problem is that making the control of inflation the sole aim of economic policy could entail very high interest rates in the transitional period, and could mean more depressed economies as a result. There is no convincing evidence one way or the other that you grow faster with low inflation or higher inflation. Switzerland has a good growth record with low inflation. Many of the Asian tigers have excellent growth records with quite high levels of inflation. Japan, in her fast growth era, had very variable rates of inflation.

What is less easy to establish is the notion that a low inflation euro would not only lower nominal interest rates but would also lower real interest rates. There is no obvious reason why this should follow. Real interest rates are influenced by many economic changes. The economy's potential, the volume of savings, the number of competing uses for those savings and the state of the public finances are all important factors in settling the long-term rate of interest. Post-war European economies have been burdened by high public sector debts building up all too rapidly. Governments have accounted for an unreasonable proportion of the savings flow in the economy, limiting the amount of money available for more productive uses. There has also been a reluctance to save in many western European economies as a result of high tax rates and the development of a welfare safety net. If people are left with very little at the end of the week or month to spend or save because the government is accounting for such a high proportion of their incomes, and if at the same time the government is making various promises to look after people if their circumstances deteriorate, the savings rate is bound to fall. Conversely, in more aggressive tiger economies the tax rates are lower, leaving people a higher proportion of their income to save, while fewer promises are made through the welfare safety net.

Reducing the long-term rate of interest in western Europe would be a good idea to promote faster growth. In order to do this, governments would have to cut back their requirement for funds and reduce their tax rates, leaving people with more incentive to save and more capacity to save. In the UK, the long-term corporate bond market has almost disappeared, whereas the government long term bond, or gilt market, was hyperactive for many years. This is a symptom of the underlying problem.

Most people would like faster economic growth. It makes paying for public services so much easier, it means you can keep down the level of taxation more readily and it promotes rising living standards. Much of the British political debate since the war has been, about how the growth rate can be lifted. Politicians of all parties have wished to find the magic ingredient or elixir which would transform Britain from a middle performer to a consistently high performer. In the first part of the post-war period, people cast envious eyes across the Atlantic to the success of the American dream. As Germany rebuilt herself from the traumas of the war, people then watched the German model with admiration. It is an irony of British economic development that it was only when the German economy had matured and was encountering its own difficulties of slow growth and rising public spending that the British interest in following the German model became more than academic.

The common thread lies behind the success of fast-growth economies around the world today, or in times past, lies in the attitude towards technological development and entrepreneurship. The climate has to be positive for new ideas to be adopted, for competing companies to arrive and establish themselves, for savers to be put in touch with investors and for the latent explosive energies of talented people to be unleashed. Too much government is always a bad thing. Fast-growth economies enjoy lower tax rates and smaller government. Indeed, a large government sector and too much government involvement always brings slower growth.

During the post-war period, a riveting forty-year-long experiment was conducted. In the east of the European continent within the Soviet Union and under its aegis, a group of economies attempted to grow more quickly than the west by a totally planned system. Penal tax rates were introduced, labour moved on the order of the government, production was planned in the minutest of detail, and savings and investments were directed to where the state felt they could secure the most positive advantage.

Well before the end of the experiment, people were clamouring to get out of the states that were controlled in this way. A wall had to be built across Berlin and the long east/west German frontier was protected by barbed wire. Soldiers were employed to shoot dead any citizen of the Communist bloc who decided enough was enough and wanted to leave. No one can deny that every advantage of state power was deployed in the interests of rational economic planning. By the end of the experiment, the result was a catastrophic failure. Although several countries in western Europe had gone a long way in the direction of state planning and high taxation, they had preserved enough of the free enterprise spirit to ensure a much higher rate of growth. Those that taxed least and intervened least grew fastest. By the end of the Communist period, the Communist states were in disarray. Their slow growth meant that their consumers had missed out on a whole new generation of products. Whereas in the west it was a typical experience to have a colour television in the lounge and a modern car in the garage, in the Communist states the typical experience was a radio or black-and-white television in the lounge with a very restricted range of programmes controlled by the government and a bicycle in front of the flat.

The single currency Social Chapter and European government scheme does not go to the extremes that the Communist project went to. The architects of western European integration genuflect to the idea that private enterprise has a role to play and that some freedoms have to be left to the subject. None the less, in the bureaucratic minds of western Europe there is an inherent tendency to believe that the state needs to intervene a great deal, that high tax and welfare spending are necessary part, of a 'caring' society, and that at the very least government has to be in partnership with free enterprise to ensure fair play and good development.

The Social Chapter is the EU's genuflection to the idea that governments should control the labour market. The origins of the poor economic growth rate of western Europe lies in these very attitudes. There are three million self-employed people in the UK. This represents a big growth in self-employment in the 1980s and 1990s as a result of the deliberate attempt to create a

117

more favourable climate for enterprise. In Britain, tax rates were cut, some of the rules and regulations were reduced or removed, and a number of markets were opened up so that new businesses could grow or get a slice of the action. New telephone companies, new bus companies, new water and energy companies have emerged through the liberalisation of those former monopolised markets.

However, there are still considerable impediments in the way of the self-employed or the small entrepreneur expanding his or her business. Once a small business reaches around £50,000 turnover a year it has to go through the elaborate and complicated process of compulsory registration for the European tax, value added tax. At once, the small businessman has to take some of his time and attention away from his customers and give them to the very detailed financial compilations and calculations. He is inundated with the myriad forms and advice and guidance notes, and has to submit regular figures to the VAT inspector. The inspector will then turn up at his premises and may again divert the entrepreneur's attention for many hours, or even days, going over his systems to make sure that every penny of potential value added tax is being properly accounted for and paid. While a business with a turnover of £100 million can handle this within the normal margin of business activity, a business with a turnover of £50,000 and one principal will inevitably have to divert attention away from customers and business development. Many decide it is not worth the hassle and deliberately limit their business size to somewhere just beneath the VAT threshold.

There are also enormous complications in the way of taking

on an additional employee. The self-employed man can just about cope with his own annual tax return, setting out how much he has earned and how much profit he has made in the past year. He can do an annual return and calculation. He can be treated as self employed for national insurance purposes and make the necessary contributions. As soon as he decides to employ one additional person, he has to run a complete pay-as you-earn system for income tax for that employee, and an employer's national insurance system. It is another formidable obstacle in the way of the entrepreneur. Many entrepreneurs are good at decorating or mending computers or writing software. They have had no training in how to account for VAT or how to ensure their employees are paying national insurance. Their prime interest in life is in the service they provide to the customer, not in the intricacies of the tax and regulatory system. Many will therefore conclude that it is not worthwhile taking on the second employee.

If Europe is serious about generating more jobs for people and thereby promoting a higher growth rate, it must tackle these type of obstacle to the development of successful small business success. The European Union seems much more interested in large business than small. Bureaucrats like big business because big business can field well-educated people speaking a similar language to the bureaucrats to attend important meetings to discuss new regulations and policy. Very often, the bureaucrats and the large companies develop an unholy alliance to defend a particular cartel, monopoly or practice against the newcomers, the challengers, the small businesses who wish to compete. Adam

Smith stated that when more than one manufacturer meet together they are often planning a conspiracy against the public. It is even truer to say that very often when European bureaucrats and politicians get together they too are planning some conspiracy against the public. They often do it for the best of motives, but they do it none the less.

In the trade and industry area of European policy, they have developed a whole family of directives to control and regulate the design of particular products. Ostensibly, this is to promote a more uniform market and to safeguard health and safety. In practice, it can become a way of reinforcing the strong position of the leading businesses in the industry and of preventing outsiders from successfully challenging. In the name of protecting employment, the European Community has increased the costs and complexity of employing people. This may offer some temporary assistance to those who are already lucky enough to have jobs, but it is very bad news for those seeking jobs, as it reduces the willingness of entrepreneurs to take on staff.

Nor is it possible to argue that saving foreign exchange dealing costs on international trade between member states who join the single currency will of itself provide a great boost to economic activity. Most businesses in the UK are small. They employ fewer than twenty employees, they sell into a local or regional market, and they do not have the time or the capacity to undertake trans-actions in foreign countries. A typical entrepreneur in Britain is not a fluent French or German speaker. It is not his natural incli-nation to get on a plane to Paris or Bonn to sell his products when his company still has not penetrated the whole of the Birmingham market. There is a natural affinity to doing business close to home, in your own language. As a result, most UK small businesses are almost entirely dependent on the domestic market for their turnover and, for the foreseeable future, will grow by widening their product range and their geographical coverage within the UK. For these businesses, there will be no savings whatsoever from the introduction of a single currency, because they are not collecting revenues or incurring costs in France or Germany.

At the other end of the spectrum, there are very large businesses who have already avoided running currency risks when trading between France, Germany and Britain. Sensible large businesses use forward markets to eliminate or reduce their currency risk. There is no need to take any risk if a business does not wish to. If, for example, British business decides to quote for a job in Germany in order to compile the quotation it will calculate the flow of Deutschmark/euro costs and revenues it will incur in order to fulfil the contract. A prudent business adds to its quotation the modest costs of forward cover to make sure it is not exposed on the net position in Deutschmarks/Euros carrying out the contract. Alternatively, the company may discover that the revenues and costs are in balance, with just the profit element remaining to repatriate into pounds. In this case, the company may well wish to quote in Deutschmarks/Euros on an uncovered basis because the costs and revenues will balance out.

Most large businesses are global not European. Even quintessentially European businesses such as Unilever and Shell, both

121

with Anglo-Dutch origins, shareholdings and main offices, are now truly global corporations. Both would argue that the dynamic growth in their business in the years to come is going to come in Asia rather than in Europe. Both would accept that much of their trading is going to be dollar-based.

In the case of an oil company, all oil is traded internatinally in dollars. The spot, or current price, and contract price of oil is settled in dollars, forward and spot markets settle transactions in dollars, and many of the costs of setting up oil wells and servicing oil installations are incurred in dollars. If British companies really wished to eliminate the most serious exchange risk, Britain would merge with the dollar bloc rather than the euro bloc. Volumes on the London foreign exchanges demonstrate that the dollar is still the dominant currency for business transactions. Unilever would concede that many of its raw materials are also priced in dollars and bought in dollars. The world's soft commodity markets, such as oil, are dollar-denominated. The advent of the euro would do nothing to stop this kind of exchange risk. Indeed, the transition from the pound to the euro would expose British businesses to bigger dollar risk, as the euro is more volatile against the dollar.

The argument for the single currency and the exchange trans-action costs comes down to an argument about the advantage of a medium-sized company with strong trading in France and Germany but not in other overseas markets. It would be possible to find examples of such British businesses, but they would be few in number and would represent a relatively small share of total British national output. These are the companies that would gain most from the single currency. Medium-sized companies are not as happy as larger companies at using forward cover and forward markets. They have a less sophisticated treasury function. They are exposed to some foreign exchange risk when trading in both francs and Deutschmarks, and they would eliminate that if the national currencies were abolished.

However, it would not be cost-free for them. While the foreign exchange dealing costs might amount to a couple of per cent, taking both the difference between buying and selling price and the commission together, the money transmission cost would often be higher than the foreign exchange transaction cost. Settling in euros still requires money transmission between Britain, France and Germany. Bank charges for money transmission services have gone up, offsetting some of the benefit of no foreign exchange charge. The Commission has been most upset by this predictable development.

At the same time, the medium-sized business would incur all the transitional costs of re-equipping if collecting money from customers directly and changing accounting systems, invoicing procedures and the like.

The idea that cutting foreign exchange costs should be the decisive argument in favour of a single currency is a very small tail wagging a very large dog. It is attacking costs in the UK that impact on less than 15 per cent of our gross domestic product. One-third of our economy is taken up with foreign trade. A little under one half of this total foreign trade in goods and services is with the European Community. In practice, the savings will be swamped by higher money transmission costs and the interest charges on the new equipment to handle the single currency. Lifting the growth rate would require materially lower interest rates. These would have to be allied to a different approach to taxation, public spending and entrepreneurship.

In a British economy with £1000 billion of total public and private debt, every 1 per cent change in the interest rate either adds or subtracts £10 billion from the spending power of people, businesses and government. This does not all flow through to increased growth, as there are losers as well as winners from changes in rates. A cut in interest rates helps the borrower, but impedes the saver. Not all of the change flows through immediately or at all as quite a lot of debt has been lent at fixed rates for a long period. None the less, the figures show that an interest rate change is far more significant than removing foreign exchange dealing costs or than the normal amounts of money moved around in tax changes in a typical budget.

We have seen the efficacy of lower interest rates generating employment and growth in both the 1980 and the 1990s. The long controlled boom of 1981–7 and the sharper uncontrolled boom of 1987–9 were both ushered in by relatively low interest rates. The contraction of the early 1990s was brought about by very high interest rates. The long recovery after 1992 was primarily the product of reducing interest rates by almost two thirds from their peak.

Critics are right to say that the swings in British interest rates have been too violent. In the early 1980s, the Conservative government inherited a very inflation-ridden economy and decided on a severe shock through interest rates to reduce inflationary expectations. It did work, but it did considerable damage to many businesses in the process. In the late 1980s and early 1990s as we have seen it was the attempt to stabilise the pound against the Deutschmark which destabilised everything else. Had we not followed the Deutschmark, we could have pursued a much more sensible monetary policy, with relatively higher interest rates in the late 1980s and relatively lower interest rates in the early 1990s with a less severe cycle. This is what we should now aim to do freed as we are of the shackles of the Exchange Rate Mechanism.

The common ground and the common sense in this debate is to look not just at the name of the currency or the institution of the Central Bank, but at the conditions which are required in any currency to create low and stable inflation and low interest rates. A good rate of growth is partly the result of a successful monetary and interest rate policy, but it is also very helpful in encouraging confidence in a currency and generating the savings necessary to keep interest rates low. In economics, nothing succeeds like success. Expectations are most important and there are strong strands of opinion and fashion concerning a country's prowess or lack of prudence.

The UK is an example of a country which has, in recent years, been able to change its image in the wider economic world. Although markets are still somewhat distrustful of British monetary policy – understandable enough given the enormities of the run-up to membership of the ERM and of the ERM era itself – markets have changed their view on many other essential characteristics of the British economy. In the 1970s markets had written off the UK. It was seen as high-cost, strike-ridden, inflexible, a technological backwater. Most of those perceptions have been radically reversed in the 1980s and 1990s.

By 1997, Britain was seen as one of the most flexible economies of western Europe. It is seen as a low-strike country with relatively good industrial relations. It is seen as a centre of technological excellence in many areas and viewed favourably by many industrial as well as commercial investors from around the world. People also believe that the political risk in the UK is low. They trust British institutions, as Britain is a rare example of a country that has survived without a civil war or revolution for 350 years. They also believe that whichever democratic party was in control, the broad outlines of policy in favour of a mixed economy and a good free enterprise sector have now been established. While Conservatives would not agree that there is little or no threat in the Labour Party, many international investors have been relaxed so far under the current Labour government. It takes time for the higher taxes and increased regulations to influence investor attitudes.

These changed perceptions are very helpful in stimulating a higher rate of growth in the UK. They mean that investors from around the world are more likely to come to Britain than they were twenty years ago. They mean that the large successful liquid London markets are able to marshal money for big British projects or British companies if they wish to develop or expand. Many now see Britain as the least objectionable part of the European Community, inside the walls of fortress Europe but not encumbered with so many manacles and foot irons. All this is slowly changing for the worse, as the UK adopts more and more of the regulatory costs and higher taxes of mainland Europe.

Raising the rate of savings in an economy can best be done by allowing the return to savers to rise. The British government has from time to time intervened to help this happen. It can readily do so by offering more tax breaks to savers. A variety of schemes have been deployed over recent years. The business expansion scheme allowed full tax relief on new risky equity investments. It has been replaced by the venture capital trusts, offering 20 per cent off the cost of any investment for the taxpayer making it. Tax-reduced savings accounts have been introduced through the ISA scheme, and the general rate of tax on savings has been lowered in line with the lower income tax rate. The special tax supplement or saving penalty under Labour in the 1970s has also been removed.

Further moves in the direction of deregulating business and cutting the tax rates on business would raise the rate of return further. These are the policy changes that have to be put through if saving is to be encouraged and enterprise flourish. If you ask a the owner of a small business what he would most like for Christmas to encourage the growth of his business, he will rarely say a single currency. He would be very likely to say exemption from VAT registration or an easier way of satisfying the Inland Revenue and the national insurance officials. Some large businesses trading abroad may well say that, among other things, they would like currency stability. If you tell them that the price of currency stability might well be interest rate instability as we demonstrated during our period in the Exchange Rate Mechanism, they would then politely say 'No thank you'.

It is a deception to suggest to people that if they abolish their national currencies there is a relatively painless way of accelerating the rate of growth by more than 1 per cent per annum and of creating prosperity on a scale we have not seen before. All the evidence shows the opposite is more likely. Preparing for monetary union so far has littered Europe with closed factories, lost jobs and redundancy notices. The crisis of unemployment across the Continent is now obvious to all but the senior politicians. The roots of the crisis lie in the very single currency scheme that is proposed as the solution. Europe has to understand that it is an area of low competitiveness and high costs. It is overburdened with too much government and too much regulation, and it fell further behind the dynamism of the Asian and American economies in the 1990s. Studying Asia would show that it is not a single currency that has fuelled the growth of Korea, Taiwan, Singapore, Hong Kong and the other emerging Asian tiger economies. Japan has never proposed abolishing the yen and joining in a new currency for the whole of south-east Asia. Countries as small as Singapore and Hong Kong preserve their own currencies and yet have achieved very high growth rates. Germany has reluctantly come round to the view that lower taxes are part of the answer to high unemployment, and is introducing a tax reduction package. Others on the Continent are also changing their ideas in this way, at exactly the same time as the UK government is substantially increasing the tax burden.

Asian commentators tell us that the source of their growth is other than currency change. Their growth has come from relatively low taxation and very dynamic enterprise. Hong Kong is a bare rock jutting into the ocean. It has no natural advantages other than the talents of the people who have come to settle there. Singapore is a large city, but a small state. It has very little spare land and no natural resources of its own. Yet just like Hong Kong, it has shown by the talents of its people that it can grow quickly and attain a good standard of living. These are the countries we should study if we wish to understand the dynamics of growth in the modern world. We should worry that the Asian tigers regularly achieve growth rates twice or three times that of the principal European economies. We should worry that the technology of America and Asia is in many fields surpassing the technology of western Europe. We should learn from Asia and America rather than seek to shut ourselves off from them. We will not get rich by protectionism. We will get rich by hard work. There is no government answer that can make us rich. We can only prosper as a people if all or most of us wish to do so and if we make our own contributions through a free-market economy.

The contrast between the tax rates in Hong Kong and Singapore on the one hand and Continental Europe on the other is very stark. In France, income tax rises to a top rate of 54 per cent. In Germany, tax rises to a rate of 53 per cent, which comes into effect for incomes of more than £36,000. Taxes are levied at more than 35 per cent on incomes above £8,500. In Italy a 45.5 per cent tax-rate comes into effect on incomes of more than £42,000. Between a quarter and a third of people's incomes that are quite low are regularly taken by Continental European countries in taxation, and over half of the incomes of more successful people. In Singapore, the top tax rate is only 30 per cent, while non-resident individuals are taxed at a flat rate of 27 per cent. Those who work in Singapore for more than 60 days but fewer than 183 days a year pay only 15 per cent tax. An individual in Singapore can earn as much as $150,000 Singapore dollars before his tax rate rises above 24 per cent.

The news is even better in Hong Kong. The top rate of tax in Hong Kong is 20 per cent. The tax rate is 2 per cent on the first HK$20,000, 9 per cent on the next HK$30,000 and 17 per cent on the following HK$30,000 of income. Hong Kong's top tax rate is less than the UK's standard rate and is less than half the top rates of tax in Europe.

The position of companies in Singapore and Hong Kong is even more favourable compared to the position of trading enterprises on the Continent of Europe. There are no capital gains taxes in Singapore, and companies pay a flat rate of tax of only 27 per cent. A large number of sources of financial income only attract a 10 per cent concessionary rate. In Hong Kong, the profits tax is levied at a rate of only 16.5 per cent, and again there is no capital gains tax. There are also generous depreciation and initial allowances.

It's little wonder that the Singapore and Hong Kong economies have grown between twice and four times as quickly as the French, German and Italian economies. The climate for business is heady in these countries. Businesses can keep most of the profit they make, often ploughing a lot of it in to new investment and taking on more people. Individuals can keep so much more of their income if they work hard. Knowing that however hard you work, the State can take only one-fifth of your total salary in Hong Kong is a much greater incentive than in France, where you know that you can keep just a little over two-fifths of anything you earn once you are paying the top rate.

The single currency for western Europe will clearly lead in due course to common taxation. That will be part of creating a single economic policy. Do we really want the people who brought us the common fishing policy and the common agriculture policy getting their hands around the necks of the whole economy? On the evidence so far, whenever the EU controls a policy it damages British interests.

The European Union often pursues policies which make the problems of local and regional dislocation worse. The most obvious example in the UK is the common fisheries policy. Before joining the European Community in 1972, Britain had a strong domestic fishing industry and had protected waters beyond her coasts which teamed with a good variety of fish. The Devon and Cornish ports, the west Welsh ports, the East Anglian ports, the Scottish ports, the Yorkshire and Lancashire ports were all most successful towns and villages. A large number of people were employed and a large number of trawlers were regularly tied up at the quayside delivering their fish.

As a result of the 1972 treaty, Britain's fishing grounds became, in the words of the EEC, "a common resource". This meant that the fishing grounds had to be open to the trawler fleets of countries such as Spain, when they joined the EEC. The

Spaniards have decided that the British fishing grounds are a common resource of great potential and have invested substantial amounts of money in large trawlers with powerful fish-catching equipment suitable for the colder, rougher northern waters around the British Isles. The sudden surge of Spanish vessels into the British fishing grounds has started to denude those fishing grounds of fish. As a result, the European Community has decided to impose limitations upon the amount of fish that anyone could catch, limiting net size, ordering the return of small fish to the sea and imposing physical quotas.

Over the years, the quota system has been progressively tightened against Britain. Thousands of trawler-men have lost their jobs and hundreds of trawlers have had to be scrapped. Visiting the British fishing ports now is a depressing experience with few of them surviving, and those that have survived operating fewer vessels.

The scheme developed its own absurdities. Small fish were to be put back in the name of conservation. The only problem was that, by the time the fish were thrown back into the sea, they were dead. Far from helping to replenish the fishing grounds it meant that further fish had to be caught from the sea in order to meet the quota of larger-size fish. It has encouraged a great deal of illegal and illicit fishing and landing, and has created a great deal of tension between the British and Spanish fishing fleets.

Under the latest proposals in 2001, Britain is expected to cut her fishing fleet under the quota system by another 40 per cent. The demands of the Spanish are so insatiable and the reduction of fish stocks so acute that it has been decided to reduce the fishing quotas still further. There is now a complete ban on fishing for cod in the North Sea, once the UK's staple fish, the mainstay of the fish and chip shop. Decommissioning targets have been drawn up to scrap vessels, and grants will be offered to those who leave the fishing industry. In 2002, the full system will be brought in, including special fishing permits. Regulation 101/76 gives the ultimate power to the authorities to control fishing vessels, to decide where the vessel may fish, the amount of fish the vessel may catch, the species, the minimum size or weight of the fish, the type of gear the fishing vessel may use, the number of vessels that can fish in any given area and the amount of time that the vessels can stay at sea.

Already, in order to comply with the regulations, many British fishing vessels are able to operate for only two or three days a week, while others have to give up fishing before the end of the year in order to stay within the quota limits. The tragedy is that the results of the common fisheries policy are visible in much-depleted fish stocks and in considerable damage to the sea-bed and to the spawning grounds of the fish. Spaniards have done similar damage to Canadian fish stocks, leading to sharp Canadian retaliation in 1994 and 1995 and general British sympathy with the Canadian position.

The decimation of the fishing industry has, of course, caused problems of unemployment and recession in the fishing towns and villages of the UK. It is but one all too obvious example of how Community policy can damage not only jobs and employment but also the social and community fabric in the affected areas. Something similar has happened in many steel areas around the Community, through the introduction of a quota system and the forced closure of a great many steel making plants. The British beef industry has suffered, too: after the outbreak of BSE led to wholesale slaughter in the late 1990s it was banned from selling any of its product any where in the world apart from the UK for many months. I have never understood how the Community could believe that British Beef is safe enough for British people to eat, but not safe enough for anyone else to eat. It implied double standards and it implied that the Community thought that looking after the interests of British people was considerably less important than looking after the interests of the French, Germans or Italians or, for that matter, South Africans and Americans. Most of the British herd had to be destroyed, and the industry was forced to rebuild at great cost. When BSE was found in Continental herds, the action was less rapid and less draconian. There has been a similar response to the outbreak of foot-and-mouth in sheep and cattle, even though this disease does not harm people.

The common agricultural policy keeps food prices in the EU well above world market prices. Quotas and controls are needed to try to prevent overproduction at these high prices. Many farmers find it worthwhile to farm intensively, forcing other areas of land to be left idle, with payments for not using such land. The common agricultural policy means intensive animal rearing and heavy use of fertilisers in places combined with quotas while leaving land fallow elsewhere. The UK is often short of quota to produce what it needs.

Policies such as these imposing quotas, limiting businesses' freedom of action, destroying industries by bans will inevitably cause more social and regional problems and will inevitably boost the demands for more cash to be spent on alleviating the consequences. The cost of offering money to farmers to slaughter their cows in Britain is prodigious; the costs to both the British national and European budgets are ultimately borne by the British taxpayer. The costs of the fishing vessel retirement scheme and the unemployment payments to the fishermen who are being pushed out of work are also now very large. By these means Europe will not only preserve her high tax levels, but will come to need even higher tax levels if these are the kind of policies the European Community is going to pursue over an ever wider range of industries.

The assertion of governmental or imperial power has always rested upon the assertion of the rights to levy taxes, to spend money and to impose a portrait of the head of the king or the authority upon the coin. The European Community is following a well-trodden path in wishing to issue and design its own coinage. The power to tax is fundamental in establishing governmental rights. It is difficult to see why British people would want a common economic policy run by the very people who brought us the common fisheries policy and the common agricultural policy. It will be even worse as the common taxation policy evolves to complement the control over interest rates, money and budgets which is a crucial part of the euro scheme.

Five problems with the common fisheries policy

1 The common fisheries policy means that Spanish and other foreign fishing fleets can come and take our fish.

2 The CFP applies only to UK waters. We cannot send our fishing fleet off to the Mediterranean to take Spanish fish.

3 Quota controls mean that we can land less than half of the fish caught from our waters. That is not enough to keep our fishing fleet in business, and means expensive fish in the fishmongers.

4 If fishermen catch too many of the wrong types of fish they throw them back dead, in the name of conservation!

5 The introduction of the CFP led to overfishing and a rapid reduction of stocks, because too many foreign boats came into our waters.

Five problems with the common agricultural policy

1 The CAP creates surplus stocks in some products, which then go to waste.

2 The CAP costs the UK household an average £16 a week more than if we bought on world markets.

3 Despite the high prices, the controls and poor management fail to help the farmers, who find it very tough.

4 The CAP fails to prevent scrapie, BSE and other problems, followed by drastic regulatory action which damages the industry.

5 The CAP encourages intensive farming methods on some land, and payments to farmers to keep other land idle to

combat over-production.

Ten errors in a common economic policy

1 There isn't one exchange rate that is right for London and Lisbon.

2 There isn't one interest rate that is right for Manchester and Marseilles.

3 You cannot have a single economic policy without a single budget.

4 There will be endless disagreements about how much European government should spend and where.

5 The poorer and richer regions are too different. The poor ones are likely to lose out.

6 There isn't a single labour market because there isn't a single language. There will be areas of high unemployment as a result.

7 There are many different telecoms, media and transport systems, making a common policy difficult to implement.

8 There is no single politicial system to take decisions and explain them to electors.

9 The European policy will be protectionist and anti-American, cutting us off from US innovation and prosperity.

10 The pensions liabilities of Continental countries are huge; Britain will be asked to pay higher taxes to help out with the problems this causes.

Chapter six

Why the EU wants taxes to go up

British enthusiasts for the single currency tell us constantly that tax policy will remain in the hands of member states and national Parliaments, even after a single currency union has been created. Yet the power to tax is rapidly being taken away by Brussels rules and regulations. We have seen how the treaty requires the new authorities to control deficits and to influence spending priorities. A single currency will mean higher European public spending and harmonised taxation. The endgame is probably to set common and high taxation throughout the Euroland area.

The Commission and some member states have already accepted that there will need to be bigger programmes to transfer money around the currency union from the more successful to the less successful areas. The European Community has regional programmes in place. Taxpayers in countries such as Germany and the UK pay more into the EC so that poorer countries such as Greece and Portugal can draw more out. Many wish to see this expanded, and more money sent on a regional basis from successful regions such as southern England to less successful regions such as eastern Germany or Sicily.

All currency unions have accepted that the common exchange rate, common interest rates and common monetary conditions they create may not be ideal for all parts of them. The larger the currency union area, and the more diverse its parts, the more tension there is in the economic system, and the more need there is to send money to the less successful areas to compensate for the wrong exchange rates and interest rates. If unemployment rises too far or too fast in the UK, one option available to British governments, and to the market if currencies are floating, is to devalue the pound, making British goods more price competitive. If, on the other hand, British goods are very competitive, markets and the authorities might decide to revalue the pound. We have seen this happening against the dollar in recent years, with the pound changing from $2 to the £1, down to $1 to the pound in the early 1980s, revalued to around $1.50 to the pound, and now falling again. The results of the devaluation against Continental currencies when we came out of the Exchange Rate Mechanism were especially favourable, ushering in a period of strong growth and good competitiveness for British products: so much so, that subsequently the pound has risen against the DM.

This strategy cannot work for individual parts of our currency union if they become uncompetitive within the UK. The contrast between the two parts of the island of Ireland is instructive. Until the late 1970s, the Republic of Ireland and Northern Ireland were part of the sterling single currency area. The Republic then decided to split away and create her own currency. The initial devaluation helped her competitiveness against the UK; subsequently, her currency rose a bit against the pound sterling. Her economy has done quite well since setting up a separate currency, for that and other reasons. She has enjoyed greater flexibility by being able to change the value of her currency against sterling, helping her trade with by far her largest trading partner. Ireland has also set aggressively lower rates of business tax, which has encouraged a large inward movement of jobs, companies and investment. In contrast, Northern Ireland has remained part of the sterling area, as part of her commitment to being part of the UK. She has not been able to devalue against the rest of the UK to become more competitive. The UK government has felt it necessary to put large subsidies into the Northern Irish economy to mitigate the problems of high unemployment.

It is true that the subsidies and the unemployment position are compounded by the troubles. The same difficulty can be seen on Merseyside, without terrorist violence. Persistently high unemployment in Liverpool cannot be solved by devaluation, so high levels of subsidy payments and transfers are made to help.

No one suggests that Liverpool should have a separate currency. In Northern Ireland, the majority community want to keep the pound as a symbol of their belonging to the UK and Irish nationalists would like a currency union with Eire as a symbol of their victory. It is a vivid illustration of the strong connection between currency issues and issues of nationhood. People elsewhere in the UK accept an obligation to pay higher taxes and transfer money to Liverpool or Belfast, because we are one country. There are not many English nationalists: those there are accept our obligations to Liverpool but would like to shed obligations to Belfast.

A European currency union has to accept obligations to all parts of the union. About 100 million people out of the total 300 million are living with considerably lower incomes and higher unemployment than in the successful parts of the euro area. These people need regional aid to help them, as they can no longer devalue or revalue there own currencies.

Immediate plans are to double the regional funds. Aid on the scale of the assistance we give to Northern Ireland or Merseyside would cost much more than that. Aid of only £1,000 a head per year extra to the poorer regions would cost £100 billion, and still leave the additional public spending well below the additional levels we give to the poorest parts of our currency union. Northern Ireland receives more than £2,000 a head extra.

Unfortunately, experience has also shown that regional aid is ineffective at curing deep-seated problems of unemployment and regional imbalance. This is unlikely to deter politicians, however. Unable to do anything about the interest rate and exchange rates that are crippling other parts of Europe, they are bound to seek subsidies. Given the record of the European institutions, they are bound to provide some: it is the way the official mind works in Europe. There is a wish to create a kind of dependency culture, where people and companies are required to feel grateful for being given back some of their own money, and where there is a great merry-go-round with some winners and some losers and the bureaucracy taking a stiff handling fee on the way.

The demands to bring tax rates into line are building rapidly. The process began a long time ago for indirect taxes. VAT was always an EC tax. The UK had to introduce it as part of its qualification for full membership. The amount of money we had to send to pay for the EC was calculated in relation to the amount of money we can raise from VAT. Subsequently, the EC issued guidelines on acceptable levels of VAT, to bring rates more or less into line around Europe. Britain has complied by raising its rates to 17.5 per cent, to bring them up to the required levels.

Leading members of the euro area and the Commission are increasingly intolerant of countries setting tax rates a lot lower than the others. It would make that part of the union very attractive to European and other businesses. They would invest there at the expense of the other areas. Rules are being developed to require income and corporation taxes within similar bands, just as VAT is now within given bands. The union has already moved to try to stop what it sees as social dumping: one member state having lower cost requirements for health, safety and employment measures to undercut others. It is now moving against "tax dumping": if one country is markedly more successful than others at keeping spending and tax low. While the more extreme powers sought by the EU backed by the French Presidency at Nice were defeated, the remorseless drive of the Union to control tax matters continued unabated, even without major treaty change.

Main rate of corporate tax in EU countries, January 1999

Austria	34%	
Belgium	40.17%	
Denmark	34%	
Finland	28%	*cont'd* . . .

France	40%
Germany	42.2%
Greece	40%
Ireland	28%
Italy	37%
Luxembourg	31.2%
Netherlands	35%
Portugal	34%
Spain	35%
Sweden	28%
UK	30%

The Irish rate falls to 10 per cent for manufacturing and many traded services. Several countries have a smaller company lower rate. In Greece, a quote on Athens Stock Exchange lowers the rate to 35 per cent, and in Germany there is a lower rate if profits are distributed.

The EU has already imposed an art market tax on auction houses, unhappy that some Continental countries had such a tax but that the more successful, British auction houses were unencumbered. The EU is seeking a common energy tax as part of its environmental strategy, and sees road tolling as a potential source of revenue. It wants a common savings or withholding tax on deposits and bonds held outside the country of the owner. There is a working party currently seeking to remove tax breaks from businesses in the interests of creating common higher business taxes around the union. The EU is making threatening noises about the low-tax offshore centres within the European geographical area, including the Channel Islands and the Isle of Man.

The Primarolo Group, ministers of the member states meeting to discuss taxation, produced a report which was submitted to the Economic and Finance Council of the EU on 29 November 1999. The group studies the impact of differing tax rates on the location of business and new investment around the EU. They concluded that "tax measures which provide for a significantly lower effective level of taxation, including zero taxation, than those levels which generally apply in the member state in question are to be regarded as potentially harmful". Member states agreed to avoid any new "harmful" tax measures in future legislation, and agreed to amend existing laws and practices to get rid of such harmful lower taxes as currently exist. They identified 66 measures which they wish to see repealed.

Ireland naturally suffered badly in this report, as it offered the best deal on taxation of any European Union country. Its special tax regime for the Dublin financial services centre, its 10 per cent manufacturing tax rate, its treatment of foreign income, the Shannon Airport Zone special tax privileges and its Petroleum tax were all listed as harmful. The UK suffered badly on behalf of its dependent territories. The Gibraltar tax regime for offshore companies and captive insurance and its general 1992 companies tax regime were deemed harmful. Guernsey was found guilty for its treatment of exempt companies, international loan business, international bodies, offshore and other insurance companies. The Isle of Man was found wanting for its taxation of international businesses companies, non-resident companies, exempt insurance companies, international loan business, offshore banking and fund management. Jersey was condemned for its rules on tax exempt companies, international treasury operations, international business companies and captive insurance companies.

In other words, the EU has decided that any territory or country that does well by offering lower taxes will be prevented from doing so in the future. The attack upon Britain's offshore islands is especially worrying. These places have built up a good business portfolio by offering lower tax rates. The island economies are bound up with offering an attractive climate for financial services and business. Some people on these islands now believe they should seek independence from the British Crown, and refuse to comply with the wishes of the EU and the British government on this most sensitive matter.

As the pressure increases to harmonise taxes, the UK and Ireland will be the countries that lose out from any such move. The UK already has a lower level of income and corporation tax than most countries on the Continent, and has kept its overall level of public spending well below most in Europe. The present Labour government is now in the process of harmonising the UK with Europe, by increasing the overall tax take sharply, and raising the proportion of national income spent by the state. Even so, the starting point was so much lower that British business and income taxes remain substantially lower than Continental rates, partly offset by higher duty payments on tobacco, petrol and alcohol.

More importantly, the UK has taken some fundamental decisions to limit future growth in our welfare bill, which has not been matched on the Continent. The UK has encouraged most people to save for their retirement through a second pension scheme. On the Continent, promissory notes have been issued, saying that larger pensions will be paid in the future, to be paid for out of tax revenues. The UK has more saved in investments for retirement than the rest of Europe put together. UK policy has also pegged increases in the basic state retirement pension to prices only, no longer to wages, cutting the growth in the cost of that scheme. In the years ahead, as a result of these decisions, there will be a growing gap between the amount of tax British people have to pay and the amount French or German people have to pay if they wish to collect the benefits they have been promised. Naturally, British people are worried that in a single currency area there might be moves to equalise these differences, expecting us to make a bigger contribution to federal revenues because we are in a much stronger tax and spending position than the others. That would only be fair, once you have accepted that you owe loyalty to the whole union.

The UK in the 1980s showed how privatisation can cut spending both through the sale proceeds and in subsequent years. A series of state pensioner companies, in need of frequent subsidies and capital support, was transferred to the private sector. Once in the private sector, far from needing government financial assistance, these companies' financial performance has so improved they actually contribute tax revenue to the budget. Other countries of western Europe will have to follow, in an effort to limit their budget requirements and their tax levels. BT, Cable and Wireless, Centrica (British Gas), PowerGen, National

Power and many others now usually pay tax and qualify for no government support. Indeed, telecom companies operating in the UK, paid £22,000 million to the government in a single year to be allowed to stay in business.

The British Chancellor of the Exchequer is already finding out the hard way how restrictive the European rules can become. In November 1999, he announced an intention to remove VAT on church repairs. He has been told that this is against European law. If he wants to go ahead, he needs not just Brussels permission: he needs to secure a change in EU VAT law. He told the House of Commons he wanted to cut Vehicle Excise Duty on British lorries, and to pay for the cut by imposing a Brit disc on Continental lorries using UK roads. Again, he has been informed that he needs Brussels approval. He was also thinking of offering business rate relief in high unemployment areas. That, too, could be done only if the EU gave the all-clear.

The last thing Europe needs is higher taxes. The single currency scheme comes from a stable of policies based on the belief in the efficacy of government. The bigger the government, so the thinking goes, the better the results. There is always another market anomaly or imperfection that they think they ought to correct. As we will see with the single currency scheme, one intervention usually leads to another, as every intervention itself distorts and throws something out of joint, necessitating further action. The scheme will undoubtedly heighten regional disparities and create big pressures for larger regional programmes. It will also bring demands to harmonise all taxation, to avoid one place stealing a march on the others.

Is there a perfect size for a currency union? Should it be as large as the USA or as small as Switzerland? Does it make sense for countries the size of Latvia to have their own currencies? Was Ireland right to split up the currency union of the British Isles? I conclude that there is no optimum size, because choosing a currency is not just an economic question, it is also a question of identity, common government and common aspirations. A currency union will only work if each person in that union accepts it is right, and accepts the responsibilities to others that it entails. It has to become an area of common taxation, to pay the bills for regional and local problems within the union.

A recent flurry of speculation has suggested that France and Germany are already working on plans for harmonised income tax. They are right to do so, given that they are serious about merging their currencies and economies. One currency will require one budget, one finance minister and one tax policy, as well as one bank, one interest rate and one monetary policy. The treaty tells us only half the story. The rest would follow as the French and German governments know only too well. The present range of income tax rates is very large and, understandably, the higher-tax countries would like to see the lower-tax ones lose some of their advantage.

Table of Income tax rates for EU countries

In descending order of combined national and local income tax rates. The tax threshold for paying higher-rate tax is in dollars. Where two countries have the same rate, the country with the lower threshold is listed above the one with the higher threshold.

	Top income tax rate	Local rate	Combined	Threshold for top rate
Belgium	55 plus 3%	7%	65%	£36,153
Netherlands	60%	0%	60%	£28,378
Denmark	28.5%	30.5%	59%	£20,276
Sweden	25%	31%	56%	£15,087
Finland	38%	17%	55%	£31,015
France	54%	0%	54%	£26,973
Germany	53%	0%	53%	£36,987
Austria	50%	0%	50%	£30,655
Spain	47.6%	0%	47.6%	£38,029
Ireland	46%	0%	46%	£7,652
Luxembourg	46%	0%	46%	£39,439
Italy	45.5%	0%	45.5%	£42,304
Greece	45%	0%	45%	£15,004
Portugal	40%	0%	40%	£18,885
UK	40%	0%	40%	£27,100

The table illustrates how high personal income taxes are in most European countries, and how low some of the thresholds are for paying higher-rate tax. Even Ireland, which has set attractive and low business tax rates and has one of the lowest higher tax rates in the EU, imposes this rate at the very low income level of $7,652 (28 September 2000 exchange rates), while several countries take more than half a person's income above $30,000.

Will we end up paying the old-age pensions for France and Germany?

In recent months, the issue of pension costs in the European Community has received a great deal of attention. From the year 2010 onwards, the number of elderly dependent on State Pensions will rise markedly. In Germany, Italy and the Netherlands, for example, the ratio of those aged over 65 to those aged between 15 and 64 is expected to rise from 20 per cent in 1990 to more than 45 per cent in 2030. This will include an increasing proportion of very old people, who will need a great deal more expensive health-care as well as pensions. In Germany, Italy, the Netherlands and Sweden by 2030, the total number of dependants taking young and old together, will rise to 70 per cent of those of working age. The Netherlands is expected to see the biggest increase, from 19.1 per cent elderly dependant in 1990 to 45.1 per cent in 2030. France sees it almost double from 20.8 per cent to 39.1 per cent, and Germany from 21.2 per cent to 40.9 per cent. The UK has one of the least dramatic increases, from 24 per cent to 38.7 per cent.

Unfortunately in countries such as France and Germany, there is considerable dependence upon state pensions which have not been funded. Conversely, in the UK, people look forward to retirement enjoying a second pension for which they and/or their employers have saved. In France and Germany, many rely upon state pensions for their livelihood. In France in 1995, public pensions cost 10.6 per cent of GDP. It is estimated that this will rise to 14.3 per cent of GDP by 2040. Similarly in Germany, the current level is 11.1 per cent and this is expected to rise to 18.4 per cent by 2040. The Dutch level is anticipated to double from 6 per cent to 12.1 per cent and the Danish level to move from 6.8 per cent to 11.6 per cent. Only the UK and Ireland have a very different position, thanks to the reliance on pensions for which people are saving. In 1995 just 4.5 per cent of UK GDP was paid in state pensions. This is expected to rise to 5 per cent by 2040. In Ireland, the percentage of GDP is expected to fall from 3.6 per cent in 1995 to 2.9 per cent in 2040. The European Community concludes:

If policies regarding benefits are unchanged and if contribution rates are not adjusted in the future, social security pension contributions would fall far short in most EU countries, implying sizeable public sector deficits and rising public debt to GDP ratios. In the meantime, real interest rates could increase, which, together with adverse debt dynamics, could trigger a snowball effect of rising debts and interest payments. In the light of these potential burdens, governments are seeking to limit social security pension commitments directly. Reforms have already been introduced in many countries, but in most cases the scale of the problem suggests that more action is needed.

Germany has recently woken up belatedly to the problem, and has announced some cuts in future pension entitlements from the state, an increase in contributions for those currently in work and paying for pensions, and the proposed introduction of a top-up scheme based on private saving and investment. It will take many years for this to begin to curb the very large future obligations, and shows how worried the government has rightly become, given the large prospective costs of the original state scheme.

The European Community is right to be alarmed. It portrays here a situation where the pensions burden keeps on rising and where countries, instead of resorting to higher taxation to pay the bills, decide to resort to borrowing. This would immediately put them outside the terms of the Stability Pact and the convergence requirements for the single currency and would, in the end become self-defeating. If a country keeps on building up its debt, it reaches the point where interest payments on the debt become too large a proportion of the state budget and of national income, leading ultimately to the bankruptcy of the state.

The UK and the Republic of Ireland are in a much stronger position because we have made private pension provision. Every month that passes sees more individuals and employers paying contributions into large pension funds. In turn good investment performances in recent years have added to the total amount of wealth available to meet future pension obligations. As a result, the UK state is not looking forward to a difficult future where the social security payments will spiral out of control.

Fear has grown in the UK that if we joined the single currency there would be a direct mechanism by which our success in paying for our own pensions could be transferred to help those in France and Germany who have not made similar provision. There is, indeed, a danger that our relative prudence would lead to us being penalised in a single currency scheme. People fear that some way will be found to tax us more to help countries with less good pension positions.

There would be no direct means of taking money out of my or your pension fund and putting it into the pockets of a French or

German pensioner. Our pension fund investments are protected by British Trust Law and we will receive our pension payments come the day of our retirement, assuming the investment managers do well and the fund is properly looked after. However, if we were in a currency union with France and Germany, the fact that their state could not meet the pension expectations of retiring French and German citizens in the next century would matter to us as well. Continental countries would expect the UK to make a larger contribution to EU costs from UK taxation, to help compensate for their difficulties on pensions. Taxes would be increased in the UK transferring the tax money from the UK to France and Germany. The UK governmant has already introduced a tax on pension funds.

The UK took some brave decisions in the 1980s to tackle the problems of growing pension bills. The Conservative government that came to power in 1979 inherited the state earnings related pension scheme, a pension scheme that topped up the standard state retirement pension. Individuals made contributions to the earnings related scheme year by year, contributions geared to the amount they were earning. In return they were offered a promise of pensions related to their final salaries on retirement. Like the standard state retirement scheme and the schemes in France and Germany, the money collected for the earnings related pension scheme was not invested or put on one side for the future needs but was spent on general Government expenditure. As a result when pensioners come to retire expecting payment of their pensions they will depend upon that future generation of taxpayers to pay money in so that they can receive their pensions payment.

In the mid-80s the Thatcher administration was persuaded that the state earnings related pension scheme would prove to be far too costly in the next century. That government took two important courses of action. First, it cut substantially the future benefit entitlements under the state earnings related scheme, before too many people had committed too much money on the basis of the old prospectus. Second, it offered a better financial incentive for people to opt out of the state earnings related scheme and to make their own provision with or without the help of their employer in a properly funded pension scheme of their own. Most people in the UK now do pay in direct to a pension scheme of their own which amasses savings on their behalf.

France and Germany need to undertake a similar type of reform. They need to tell their citizens that they cannot meet all of the pensions promises that have been made in recent years. They need to offer a framework in which French and German people know that they too have a pool of assets they can turn to when they are elderly.

If we join a currency union with countries that have failed to take this necessary action, we will be asking for trouble. Despite the Thatcher reforms in the field of pensions provision, social security in the UK has continued to grow dramatically in the 1980s and 1990s. Between 1979–80 and 1995–6 means-tested benefits and payments for sickness and invalidity have grown by almost 5 per cent of GDP at a time when GDP itself has been expanding quite rapidly. Without the pensions reform, the whole edifice would soon have become cripplingly expensive and top heavy. Even the UK needs further reforms in its social security system to ensure proper control over public spending and borrowing. The problem is much worse in all of the other EC countries, save the Republic of Ireland, as revealed by the figures on social security and pensions.

The impact of all this on government debt levels and interest payments is very marked. In the case of Greece, interest payments on government debt alone now amount to 11.9 per cent of total gross domestic product, and in Italy it is 10.5 per cent. Belgium at 8.5 per cent and Sweden at 7.5 per cent also have cripplingly high interest burdens to bear. Given that public spending is around or under half of total national income, it means that in these countries around one-fifth of their total public spending is now absorbed merely by paying interest bills on borrowings they have already incurred. The rakes progress has been dramatic in several countries. Even in low-borrowing countries such as France, the debt build-up in the 1990s has been colossal. In 1991, French government debt was only 35.8 per cent of GDP; now it is 56.4 per cent. Finland has seen it almost treble from 23 per cent in 1991 to 61.3 per cent now, and Sweden has seen an increase from 53 per cent to 78.1 per cent. Even the UK, with a relatively low level, has seen it grow from 35.7 per cent to 56.3 per cent between 1991 and 1996. It has since reduced as a result of substantial tax increases after 1997.

The bankers at Maastricht are right to worry about government debt levels. The politicians are right to worry about the policies it would require to correct the deficits when economies are performing badly or are in recession. The ultimate solution is to reform social security and pensions in many of these countries. This will be a long and painful process. It holds no immediate prospect of these countries meeting the Maastricht requirements for the single currency, but it does hold out a medium, to long-term prospect of better discipline and more economic success if they do so. The danger at the moment is that they will take panic measures that are unacceptable politically and will do damage economically in their vain pursuit of the Maastricht requirements.

Advocates of the euro should explain to people that in any currency union it is one for all and all for one. The UK should want to make a bigger contribution to the poorer parts of the union if we went in. They acknowledge that the EU is a high tax areas and are proud of it. Our taxes will go up if we join in. The EU will need more money to spend, and it will make it more and more uncomfortable for any country that wants to keep its tax rates low.

Ten reasons why the euro means higher European taxes

1 Euro-zone leaders say it will not be fair if one member state has lower taxes than another – they must be harmonised upwards to stop one or two countries attracting too much investment at the expense of the others.

2 They want a common environmental policy that tries to tax pollution – that means a common European energy tax.

3 They want to stop people putting money on deposit in

another country to avoid tax – that means a common European savings or witholding tax.

4   They want VAT to be the first truly European tax, with rates and incidence set by the EU and the tax collected by the EU.

5   They have imposed an EU Art Market Tax – which is pushing business out of EU auction houses to other countries altogether.

6   They are seeking common road tolls.

7   A currency union requires the richer places in it to send money to the poorer areas. That will mean higher taxes to pay for the transfers.

8   They want to stop cross-border fraud, so they will take wide-ranging powers to interfere in tax matters.

9   They have a working party devising ways to stop countries offering corporate tax breaks or lower rates than other countries.

10 In the 2000 pre-Budget statement, the British Chancellor announced lower vehicle excise duty, the end of VAT on church repairs, lower stamp duty in the inner cities and a possible selective reduction in business rates. All of these ideas require Brussels approval. He had to back down on three of them.

Chapter seven

Why the City of London has to remain offshore from the euro

One of the most commonly used arguments in favour of the single currency for Britain is the belief that the City of London will only survive as one of the world's and Europe's leading financial centres if the UK joins the euro. Those in favour of a single currency say financial business will move from London to Frankfurt if the UK stays outside. Some in the City also believe this, saying that if a single currency is going to take place, Britain must be part of it, must join in, must influence it, must be enthusiastic about it.

This view is encouraged strongly by the French and Germans. They have long since wished to challenge London's pre-eminence as a financial centre in western Europe. They are also very keen to draw Britain into the single currency scheme. They regularly argue that because London is excluded from the single currency scheme it will be bad news for the London markets. Sometimes it is difficult to understand why they are worried about this, given that one of the main aims of their policy is to try to move business away from London to Frankfurt and Paris. One can't help but think that maybe they protest so strongly about

London's interests because they secretly believe that joining the single currency would be bad news for London and would help them fulfil their aim of redirecting business from Britain to France and Germany.

London is the pre-eminent financial centre of western Europe. Indeed, it is one of the world's big three financial markets. The City of London is pre-eminent worldwide in foreign exchange dealings. More than two-thirds of all foreign currency dealings worldwide take place through the London markets: it is bigger than New York and Tokyo combined. The same is true of dealings in shares outside the country of origin of the company concerned. London again has accounts for more business than Tokyo and New York combined. In banking, London is no longer so dominant, but it is considerably bigger than most European centres and still ranks as one of the important banking centres of the world. More than five hundred international banks are congregated in the City of London. The City is famed for the excellence of its banking staff and for the innovatory qualities of its leading bankers. London has a prominent position in the provision of business and financial services and is a very large investment management centre. London is also famous for its legal and consultancy services, servicing a large market in the English-speaking world and in all those countries with common-law traditions. Many Commonwealth countries and the USA have legal systems based on precedent, different from the codified, Continental system.

It is important to understand why London has flourished as a financial centre in the post-war period before answering the question: "What impact would the single currency have upon London one way or another?" In the nineteenth and early twentieth centuries, London rose as a large financial centre because it was banker to the empire. In the early days of industrial capitalism, Britain was ahead of her competitors in Europe and in America. She generated substantial surpluses and accounted for a large proportion of world trade. As a result, London, Liverpool and Bristol became the centres for shipping, freighting and trade services. London was the pre-eminent centre to finance trade, undertake currency dealings and provide a market in the principal commodities ranging from gold and silver through the soft commodities to industrial products. London's success was based upon the important position of the British economy in the world economy, on the significance of trade within the empire and on its strong position in Transatlantic trade.

In the post-Second-World-War period, British industrial and commercial pre-eminence waned quite rapidly, but the importance of London as a financial and business centre did not. British governments seemed to conspire very often against the City of London. Sterling was frequently a weak and vulnerable currency. The government often imposed controls on transactions to and from sterling in an effort to buttress the pound. Britain watched as the almighty dollar conquered the world and then as the German industrial renaissance got under way, strengthening the German economy.

However, the City of London managed to detach itself from the weakness of the rest of the British economy. City experts were able to create a kind of offshore City economy dealing and trading with the rest of the world whatever the weaknesses of the domestic economy or the shortfalls and misgivings of government economic policy. If world trade and commodities were to be primarily denominated in dollars, then London accepted this and became an important dollar centre. If British citizens were prevented from going abroad spending large sums of money, then the City of London would deal for foreigners who were freer to move money around the world. If British industrial shares were no longer the right place to invest people's money, then the City of London would gain expertise at investing people's money in American, Japanese or German shares. If the British economic growth rate wasn't sufficient then the City of London would make its living by backing the American and Asian economies that were growing so much more rapidly.

In the post-war period, Britain benefited from the talent attracted from central Europe during the troubled period of the 1930s and 1940s. It was immigrant talent that founded many of the great merchant banks of twentieth-century London. They found in London a toleration of their attitudes and business practices that they could not find, or did not think they would find, on the Continent, which was being reconstructed from the ruins of the Second World War.

While the City of London often suffered from domestic government economic policies that were far from ideal, it did benefit from a long tradition of political and democratic stability: people knew that contracts would be honoured, their money would not be misappropriated or stolen, and that there were basic traditions of honesty. They also benefited from governments of all dispositions being prepared to tolerate less regulated business on behalf of foreigners than the regulations they often imposed on domestic activities. Taxation in the 1960s and 1970s was a penal 98 per cent on income from savings for investors domiciled in the UK, but these rates did not apply to foreigners investing their money through London or depending on London's investment management skills.

London also used the contacts and advantages that empire, Commonwealth and the English language brought with them. London banks and finance houses built important businesses in the former imperial territories such as Singapore and in the crown colony of Hong Kong. Through Hong Kong and Singapore they had important investment windows on the entre-preneurial east. Just as British fund managers in the early twentieth century had seen the dynamism of the United States and set up investment trusts to exploit these opportunities, so in the post-war world British investment managers saw the vitality of the Japanese economy early and many made successful invest-ments or built important businesses in the Japanese world. Britain preserved her strong links across the Atlantic. The sterling/dollar rate was an essential part of the western financial world, with Wall Street and London watching each other with great interest.

The surge of inward investment into London in the 1980s added to the strength of London as a financial centre. The decision to deregulate the City in a process known as Big Bang transformed it rapidly. The City had grown up as a club of business people coming from similar backgrounds and sharing common attitudes, probity and honesty in their business dealings. In the 1980s, small entrepreneurial businesses owned by groups, partners or directors were transformed by huge injections of foreign capital and a large number of takeovers. The City moved on from being a self-regulating group of highly competitive small businesses to being a market dominated by very large and sophisticated international banks and investment houses bringing foreign capital to add to the native talent recruited in Britain.

The City managed to get through these changes in reasonable shape. British and foreign talent found that by working together they could make an even bigger impact. When allied to substantial amounts of capital, the world was definitely their oyster. The City preserved its excellence as an innovator, launching many of the new financial ideas that generated large amounts of revenue in the 1980s and 1990s. It was in the City of London that privatisation first took root and took off. It was in the City of London that many of the new-style zero-coupon drop-lock and index-linked bonds were pioneered. It was in the City of London where the eurobond market had its day, and in the City of London where many of the financial futures instruments were first tailored alongside their American competitors.

The thesis that all this would be jeopardised if Britain does not abolish the pound is a difficult one to understand. London has grown up because of its history, because of the talents of the people involved and because its cost structure is favourable against the revenues its talents can command. It is not held back by the denomination of domestic business in pounds, even though the pound is now a comparatively small currency compared with the range and reach of the dollar and the yen. The City of London trades primarily in dollars. Whether it be oil or cocoa, gold or iron, or many bonds or many financial futures, they are all dealt in dollars. Converting the domestic currency base from the pound to the euro would make no difference to all the dollar trading. If London remains successful, it will be primarily a series of dollar-driven markets.

The theorists who favour monetary union suggest that the most important type of business that London currently transacts is government business, and that this government business would naturally gravitate to the centres handling euro business rather than sterling business. Since the euro was launched as a business currency at the beginning of 1999, there has been no such flight of activity from London to Frankfurt. The rules of competition still apply. People in Paris and Frankfurt still value the dealing abilities and terms of dealing in London and transact quite a lot of their euro business through London. British government business is still conducted through London in sterling.

If Britain had abolished the pound, then the business that is currently conducted by the British banking system and the Bank of England would be conducted under the instructions not of the Bank of England, but of the Frankfurt Central Bank. In this circumstance London might have to fight a little bit harder to preserve its role in central banking transactions – but again, if the costs were similar there would be no reason why London could not keep the business.

The argument seems to come down to the threat of protectionism. This has been made explicit when it comes to the settlement system. When the European Community worked out a new settlement system for transactions in euros, some threatened that London could not be part of this system. Common sense prevailed, and the UK can settle euro transactions after all. This most extraordinary protectionist idea of barring a member country of the European Community from a say in the business of settling in one of the currencies within the European Community was taken seriously for a while.

Anything short of such a blatant and illegal move is unlikely to succeed in damaging the business of the City of London. If London can offer more attractive dealing rates facilities in euros than Frankfurt or Paris, then it can continue to command a decent level of business. If it cannot do so, then of course it will not, but exactly the same would apply to continuing business in Deutschmark, and French francs. The issue of which currency happens to be the chosen currency of the UK is scarcely relevant to the success or failure of a world trading and financial centre on the scale of London.

If we look at the impact of the single currency on different segments of London's business, the pattern becomes much clearer. In the case of foreign exchange transactions, everyone must agree that abolishing the pound, franc and Deutschmark is marginally disadvantageous to the City of London. The City of London at the moment has an important and big business in switching between francs, Deutschmarks and pounds. If all three of these currencies were removed and replaced by the euro then the foreign exchange business between the three big western European currencies would cease. Fortunately, for the City of London, most of its business is switching between the European currencies, the dollar and the yen. There would still be very active markets switching between the euro and the yen and the dollar, as well as between the dollar and the yen.

Investment management business would also be little disturbed by the decision either to join or not to join the euro. London is a huge international investment management centre, with a large range of assets and clients from Asia and America as well as from Europe. Whether the shares of French and German companies are denominated in euros or Deutschmarks and francs makes little difference to this business. If British shares were denominated in euros rather than pounds, that too would be a matter of indifference to the investment managers, who would still have to make difficult decisions about which country, which market and which companies, although their currency judgement would be easier with respect to French, German and British investments, as there would be only one risk rather than three. There is a danger that London's big dollar business would become more risky, as the euro gyrates more wildly against the dollar than the pound does.

People in financial futures markets would lose but modestly from the transition from the pound, Deutschmark and franc to the euro. New financial futures instruments are being generated in euros instead of DMs, francs and the other member states currencies. Bonds and financial instruments denominated in euros will replace bonds in the different European currencies.

There will be some modest net loss of business as a degree of complication and the number of cross-rates that need protecting are reduced with the number of European currencies. There will be fewer deals in financial futures as rates between Euroland currencies are removed.

The impact on business consultancy, legal services and merchant bank advisory work would also be very difficult to discern. London primarily earns its living by advising in common-law and English-speaking areas. This would remain true whether the domestic currency were the pound or the euro. The main takeover markets and the bid-and-deal merger and acquisition work would also be unaffected by a change to the euro.

The supporters of monetary union concentrate primarily on monetary instruments traded by central banks and governments rather than on the bulk of private sector work. Most city revenues are private sector. Most of them come from individuals and companies placing money for investment management in personal equity portfolios and pension funds. Much of it comes from companies seeking to take each other over or from raising money for companies that would go on whatever the currency of denomination. Government work rests on raising the money through bond issues to finance the activities of governments and some currency transactions in connection with managing the reserves.

There would be some loss of business from governments in general if countries joined the euro and stuck to the Maastricht scheme. It would usher in an era of much lower public deficits and, in due course, a smaller weight of refinancing as government bonds expire and need to be replaced. If, however, this led to more company borrowing as government left more space in the markets which might be occupied by more private sector activities. If it took place against the background of the deflationary policies we have seen in preparation for monetary union, then it is quite true that there would be an overall loss of business for London and other European markets as a result of less deficit financing, fewer bond issues and a lower general level of private as well as public sector economic activity.

Such losses would not be specific to London, but would affect all the financial sectors on the Continent as well. The issue seems to revolve around whether or not London could maintain a strong position in monetary instruments and monetary control if it either did or did not participate in the Frankfurt Central Bank. As we have seen, it is more likely that London will retain its pre-eminent position in handling British government debt and British monetary instruments if Britain maintains a separate debt financing and monetary system. If Britain abolishes the pound and transfers the foreign exchange reserves to Frankfurt and follows the policy of the Frankfurt Central Bank, then it will be a bit more difficult for the City of London to retain her pre-eminent position, but if her competitiveness is not impaired then it should be all right.

The biggest threat to the City comes from changes to the regulatory framework if sovereignty passes from the British Parliament and Bank of England to the officials of the Central Bank in Frankfurt. One of the reasons why Frankfurt has not challenged London successfully in financial services and financial markets is the regulatory system that the German Central Bank has pursued over the German banking system. Some British commentators in the 1960s and 1970s thought our financial system compared unfavourably with the German one. They felt that a limited number of very large banks pursuing very close relationships with German industrial companies was ideal, and that the failure to do this in Britain accounted for the decline of some British engineering industries. This was not an entirely satisfactory explanation for the big difference in industrial performance. It took no account of the appalling strike and employee relations record in the UK compared with Germany. It did not look at the reasons why British engineering companies, especially in the motor industry, failed to design the type of products people wanted to buy, whereas the German industry was rather more successful at doing this in the 60s and 70s. But even allowing for some truth in the proposition that the German banks were better for German industry than the British ones were for British industry, it did not look at the other side of the equation where the German banks fell further and further behind in offering a wider array of financial services to business and individuals at home and abroad.

Where the German banks built strong equity and loan positions in a limited number of larger German industrial companies, the British banks and financial institutions were servicing the world, offering advice on bids and deals, investment management services, raising money through bond issues and equity financings, organising placings and innovating in ways in which traded securities could be used to finance both world trade and world industry. Britain and Britain's financial institutions had to look beyond British shores because British industry was not large enough and did not know how to use the money productively and profitably enough to sustain the appetites of the City of London.

German banks were over-regulated, limiting their scope as innovators and restraining them from becoming financiers to the world. Germany did not develop the breadth, depth and liquidity of the London capital markets and was unable to offer the fine rates and massive financial support which the London stock and bond markets provided. The development of professional investment management for many larger pension funds in Britain gave the City a further boost.

The danger for Britain in joining the single currency scheme lies primarily in the regulatory approach that the European Central Bank might operate, which could well be against the interest of the City of London. We have already seen moves in this direction through the banking and investment services directives. Early drafts of the investment services directive would have made the London system of share trading illegal. The banking directives and investment services directives are already requiring higher reserve ratios than has been the normal practice in British banks and financial institutions, lowering the return on capital and reducing flexibility of those institutions. The Frankfurt Central Bank may pursue a very restrictive policy towards financial service innovation and banking liquidity. If the international city fell under this regime as well as the domestic city committed to the euro, then it could spell disaster for the City of London.

Under a Frankfurt Central Bank and the euro regime, the City's best course of action would be to go offshore. It would need to segregate its Asian, American and African business from its European business and make sure that it was outside the regulatory ring of the Frankfurt bank. Continental regulation is stylised by proscription rather than being permissive. To get new products approved often requires a huge amount of paperwork and a long wait. Some of this is already coming into the British system by courtesy of the financial services directives that we have agreed in the name of a single market.

The question is whether the City of London could go offshore and preserve its flexibility for overseas business if Britain had joined the euro. It will require very detailed negotiations with our European partners if we wish to ensure both that Britain joins the single currency and that the City of London is not damaged by involvement in the Frankfurt regulatory system for its offshore activities. It would be possible to enjoy a system whereby London was free to undertake investment management, corporate finance, banking and other financial transactions for countries, businesses and individuals outside the European Union untrammelled by Frankfurt controls. It is more likely, however, that the architects of the single currency scheme will see in it a device for extending Frankfurt and European controls over the lucrative business of the City of London conducted outside the European Community.

The European Union could restrict the amount of bank lending the British banks could do on the grounds that it would be part of the general euro liquidity. They could also restrict foreign currency lending by British banks on the grounds that it might damage their balance sheets and overstretch them, thereby jeopardising their euro operations as well. While the European Community is pledged to freedom of capital movement within the European area, it could also impose restrictions or capital controls on movements outside the union area. This would be very damaging to the investment management business of London if it came under that particular regulation. There could also be more oppressive business rules even than the current ones drawn up as part of the single market programme. The Frankfurt bank could prevent certain types of products or investment activity. It could restrict certain types of investment advice or insist on particular financial requirements and regulations in order to undertake certain types of financial business.

The essence of the City of London is a competitive international marketplace where many new companies and activities are established week by week, jostling alongside the larger and well-established businesses already there. Too much regulation could frighten off the footloose international investors from Asia and America, and it could limit the scope for new businesses to be established to challenge the existing players. The European Community has to remember that investment and business is now foot-loose in the modern world. It is all too easy for people in Tokyo or New York or the other Asian and American centres to decide that the regulatory system has become too tight in London or Frankfurt and to direct their businesses to new offshore centres. The biggest threat that the City of London faces is not from Frankfurt, or even from Tokyo, but from the offshore centres in places such as the Bahamas. Such offshore centres will offer lower taxes and less regulation, which will attract more and more business.

For a number of years, both Frankfurt and Paris have had plans to wrest preeminence away from London to themselves. It has not only been regulation that has stood in their way. Both France and Germany have become high-cost parts of the world. The combination of building costs and staff costs is added to by the burden of high social security charges and the results of the Social Chapter on employment practices. One London-based banker working for a German business explained to me that when they had been taken over by the German bank, they had looked to see if there was anything that they currently did in London which they could transfer to Frankfurt as a token of goodwill. They soon discovered that under German rules staff were not allowed into the office building between 5.00 on a Friday evening and 8.00 on the following Monday morning. In London, people were used to working on deals or investment transactions across the weekend if necessary. The bank immediately decided it could not jeopardise its business by moving to a city where working hours were so restricted. It was a symbol of the difference between the Anglo-Saxon deal-related culture and the more regulated social culture of the Continent. Imposing Continental controls on London would not sustain the City's preeminence. It would undermine it.

So would imposing the full EU tax agenda on the City. If the City is to do as well in the twenty-first century as it did in the twentieth, it needs to be supported by low taxes as well as light regulation. Increasing stamp duty, imposing an auction house tax, putting in place a withholding tax and increasing overall corporate taxes will be bad news. So will the growing moves to block contested takeovers, the source of much of the vitality of Anglo-Saxon capitalism, and the source of excellent fees for the City of London.

Ten reasons why the euro is bad for the City

1   The City will lose all of its sterling/euro business, and all its specialist sterling activities.
2   The London-based banks will come under the same banking regulation as Frankfurt and Paris, which has held those centres back in the past.
3   The euro will lead to higher taxes, especially on savings, which will damage London's business.
4   If the dollar:euro rate continues to swing wildly, as it has so far, it will make the huge dollar business of London more difficult to maintain.
5   Adopting EU social and employment regulations will damage the City's flexible approach to employment, working hours and social regulation.
6   The London markets will lose handling UK government sterling debt.
7   Adopting the euro will lead directly to over-regulation of investment and corporate business, which will drive more of it offshore.

8   Plans to drive taxes up in low tax centres such as the Channel Islands and the Isle of Man will drive that business to Asia or the Caribbean, which means a big loss of related business for London.

9   The attitude of mind of the Continental market supervisors and market makers is hostile to the English-speaking world and markets that are Britain's traditional source of strength.

10 Britain is being drawn into trade wars with the USA thanks to the anti-American attitude of some Continental partners. This could spill over into retaliatory measures which damage the big cross-Atlantic financial business flows.

Chapter eight

The changeover

The timetable

January 2001	Greece joins single currency scheme
March 2001	Beginning of compulsory dual pricing for smaller Greek companies
July 2001	French and Belgian retail banks convert customer accounts into euro
August 2001	German mail order begins euro pricing
September 2001	euro cash supply to banks and retailers begins
From September 2001	Recommended utility bills in euros
October 2001	Dual pricing becomes compulsory for Austrian companies
December 2001	euro coin starter kits available to general public
From 1 January 2002	National currencies can no longer be used in non-cash form. euro notes and coin are gradually introduced

| 28 January 2002 | National currency ceases to be legal tender in the Netherlands |
| February 2002 | End of legal tender status for most other national currencies in euro zone |

The treaty is most detailed on how member states should move from having fifteen separate national currencies to one single currency. The second stage of the transition began on 1 January 1994. By that date, every member state had to remove capital restrictions permitting the free movement of monies between member states and with the outside world. They also had to put forward budgetary and economic plans to achieve low inflation and sound public finances. They were particularly requested to avoid excessive government deficits and were required to commence a process leading to the independence of each national central bank.

The European Monetary Institute was set up, replacing the old Committee of Governors of Central Banks. The Council of the European Monetary Institute consisted of a president and the governors of the national central banks. The EMI enjoyed a series of powers and tasks. It had to strengthen co-operation between the national central banks; strengthen the co-ordination of the monetary policies of the member states with the aim of ensuring price stability; monitor the functioning of the European monetary system; hold consultations falling within the competence of the national central banks and affecting the stability of financial institutions and markets; take over the tasks of the

European Monetary Co-operation Fund and facilitate the use of
the ecu, overseeing its development and the smooth functioning
of the ecu clearing system.

For the preparation of the third stage, the EMI shall: prepare the instruments and procedures necessary for carrying out a single monetary policy
in the third stage; promote the harmonisation, where necessary, of the
rules and practices governing the collection, compilation and distribution
of statistics in the areas within its field of competence; prepare the rules
for operations to be undertaken by the national central banks within the
framework of the ESCB; promote the efficiency across border payments;
supervise the technical preparation of ecu banknotes. The European
Monetary Institute acting on a two thirds majority of its Council members
has the power to propose opinions or recommendations on monetary and
exchange rate policy introduced in each member state.

Immediately after the third stage, the decision was taken to set
up the European Central Bank. The EMI was liquidated. Member
states joining the single currency decided unanimously the
conversion rates:

at which their currencies shall be irrevocably fixed and at which irrevocably fixed rate the ecu shall be substituted for these currencies, and the
ecu will become a currency in its own right. This measure shall by itself
not modify the external value of the ecu. The Council shall, acting
according to the same procedure, also take the other measures necessary
for the rapid introduction of the ecu as a single currency of those member
states.

In the aftermath of the destruction of the narrow-band
Exchange Rate Mechanism, a great deal of reinterpretation was
undertaken. The ecu was dumped, as its history of losing value

against the DM was an embarrassment. Apologists for the single currency now say that the question of what the new currency should be called was always left open in the treaty and could be settled at a later date. At subsequent meetings after a great deal of wrangling about whether the single currency should be called the florin or the schilling or the euro mark/euro franc/euro pound or the ecu or something else, the member states finally agreed to call it the euro.

Some have seen in the change of name the advantage that it now appears that the failure of the member states, currencies to stay in line roughly with the ecu no longer matters to the success of monetary union. Although the main emphasis of the treaty is on bringing currencies into alignment with one another, the failure of the ERM led directly to the invention of a new currency to be called the Euro, which the member states have gone ahead with despite the words of the treaty.

The handling of the transitional period has been dogged by misjudgement and bad luck throughout. Having decided to abandon all pretence at bringing exchange rates into line by narrowing the fluctuation bands, the member states and officials have turned instead to concentrating on the convergence of budget deficits. There is every reason to do this, as all will be borrowing in the same currency at an identical or very similar interest rate once the single currency has been established. Even this proved to be far more vexatious than the framers of the treaty imagined. They expected the background to be reasonable growth and prosperity in the European economies as a whole. They imagined that holding every country to a maximum level of borrowing of 3 per cent of its national output would be comparatively easy. Certainly, the Germans never anticipated that they themselves would find it difficult, if not impossible, to get their budget deficit down to the required level of the treaty.

In 1992, the single market of the European Community formally reached maturity. Many European politicians believed the hype surrounding this development. It was confidently said at the time that the creation of the single market itself would add 3 per cent to European national income on its own. This would have represented a colossal increase in national income and wealth, and would indeed have been a well worthwhile achievement. Unfortunately, the formal advent of the completed single market saw not a sudden surge in the growth rate, but a downturn in the growth rate across Europe, which took a long time to recover. I do not blame the single market for the drop in the growth rate, nor do I think that without the advent of what they called the single market the European economies would have fallen 3 per cent more.

The whole single market scheme was ill conceived and over-egged. Removing restrictions and barriers to trade between the companies and peoples of western Europe will indeed increase the growth rate and prosperity level. Many European politicians instead saw the single market policy as an opportunity to increase the powers of European central government by a huge raft of new legislation and regulation. Some of this, far from increasing prosperity and removing barriers, created new obstacles and new barriers and was damaging to prosperity. A large number of the directives took the form of prescribing in law and regulation how individual products could or could not be made. Legislators said this would help the single market because it meant that every factory and company in western Europe would make to the same standard permitting customers a wider choice of which producer supplier them the goods. It also meant that the ability to innovate and keep up with the newest technology was stifled. It became illegal in western Europe to develop certain types of new technology or to change or improve products in certain ways. Far from promoting faster growth and prosperity, in some sectors this became a modest deterrent to it. Similarly, in financial services, measures that were presented as necessary to allow a customer in Germany to buy a British insurance policy, or vice versa, rapidly became ways of increasing the general regulatory burden on all insurance companies across western Europe. Far from lowering costs and sharpening competition, they became methods of raising costs and creating new barriers to new competition.

As a result, the final completion of the legal framework of the single market was probably at best neutral for its impact on European growth. The reason the run-up to the single currency scheme was dogged by low growth and rising budget deficits lay in the Exchange Rate Mechanism and the monetary policies it required.

Although the Exchange Rate Mechanism itself did not work and had to be fundamentally revised to permit much wider bands, even these wider bands acted as a considerable restraint on the monetary policies of various member states. The most intense damage was done when the bands were narrow. In a desperate effort to keep currencies such as the franc, peseta and lira within the system, the authorities in those countries had but one choice. They had to keep interest rates higher than would otherwise have been desirable. They had to intervene actively in foreign exchange markets, selling other currencies and buying their own. As we have seen in a previous chapter, such intervention serves to reduce money supply in the home territory at exactly the same time that higher interest rates are also serving to reduce monetary growth.

It will be recorded as one of those ironies of history that a system designed to create a virtuous cycle of reasonable growth, low inflation and expanding prosperity succeeded in creating a vicious cycle in every respect save the reduction of inflation. The Germans got their way. Controlling inflation became not only the main but in effect the only economic goal being pursued. Domestic politicians in France, Spain and Italy came under increasing pressure to do something about joblessness and low growth, but on each occasion they turned their face against the adversity of their peoples and decided that the ideological drive to a single currency and low inflation was more important.

In 1998, the member states met under the chairmanship of the UK, which held the European Union Presidency at the time, to decide which countries would enter the euro. As no member state had met all of the requirements of the treaty, and as both France and Germany were having problems with the debt requirements, the stage was set for the member states to take a generous view of their achievements so far. It was resolved that every country that wished to enter, with the exception of Greece, could go ahead, whatever the figures and whatever the treaty may say. The Member states solemnly bound themselves to the single currency project, and settled the exchange rates at which they would enter the new currency.

Twelve wanted to go ahead and eleven were allowed to. The UK decided to use its opt-out and not join. All major political parties in the UK have offered a referendum before trying to join, and the government is reluctant to go to the country on the issue because of the unpopularity of the Euro. Denmark also had an opt out following the government's defeat in a referendum on the original treaty of Maastricht. An unrepentant government then put joining the euro to a further referendum and lost, so Denmark remains out of the scheme. Sweden does not have an opt-out, but the government decided that it was very unpopular with the electorate and so it was granted permission to delay its entry. Greece sought entry, but was so far out on all of the numbers that she was asked to serve a longer apprenticeship at a devalued rate in the Exchange Rate Mechanism. Ireland was allowed a small revaluation. The other countries were admitted at their Exchange Rate Mechanism mid-rates.

Entry rates into the euro, for the euro eleven and Greece

Belgium	40.3399 Belgian francs
Germany	1.95583 DM
Spain	166.386 pesetas
France	6.55957 francs
Ireland	0.787564 Irish pounds
Italy	1936.27 lire *cont'd . . .*

183

Luxembourg	40.3399 Belgian francs
Netherlands	2.20371 guilders
Austria	13.7603 schillings
Portugal	200.482 escudos
Finland	5.94573 markka
Greece	340.75 drachma

In the first two years following these decisions, things went smoothly in each country about to join, because very little happened. The idea behind the scheme was for a phased introduction, so the shock of the new would not be too great. The introduction of joint pricing over a long period was meant to accustom everyone to values in the new currency. The ability to take out a euro bank account, to carry out transactions in Euros using cheques, credit and debit cards, and the propaganda campaign for the new currency were all designed to ensure a significant number of euro transactions long before notes and coins were introduced.

However, a tidal wave of apathy hit the Continent. The November 2000 Bank of England report on euro preparations indicated that only 3.2 per cent of all transactions in euroland were taking place in euros, indicating a low level of interest and take-up by most businesses and individuals. The total value of transactions is much higher in Euros, reflecting the take up predominantly by large companies undertaking bigger deals. Only one percent of all individual transactions are undertaken in Euros, showing that it has not caught on at all with the retail customer.

The European Commission has become alarmed by the apathy. It means there will be a bigger shock to the system when it is illegal to carry on buying and selling in national currencies at the end of 2001. The Commission is now urging larger companies to pay their staff in Euros earlier than the end of the last transitional year, and urging utility companies to bill in Euros to give customers more exposure to the idea. The French and Belgian banks have also responded to Commission overtures with a proposal that they convert all their customers six months early unless those customers object.

Many in Euroland still seem to think that the euro is only going to be a parallel currency, an alternative for those who want it. They will get a surprise when their bank account is converted by compulsion and their national currency is withdrawn from circulation. It is a big disappointment to euro enthusiasts that people have been so slow to respond. It seems to indicate that most people in Euroland do not regard the euro as a good idea, as they are unwilling to use it until they are forced to. Most small businesses regard it as a cost and a nuisance and are putting off doing anything until the last minute. Some larger firms have embraced it more willingly, and use it more regularly for cross border transactions. If anything, it is a fat cat's currency, not a people's currency.

Just as individuals have been reluctant to have anything to do with the new currency, portfolio and direct investors have been rushing to the exit doors of Euroland altogether. In the ten months to the end of October 2000, there was a net outflow of 106.3 billion euros from the Euroland area to other countries. This was a little less than in the same period in the previous year when the outflow was a massive 136.9 billion

185

euros. Throughout the first two years of the Euro's life its remorseless decline reflected the way the big business backers of the euro in Europe were busily undermining it by their actions. They were keen to invest anywhere but in Euroland, and were busily sending large sums of money abroad. Since January 2001 the euro has rallied and portfolio investors have been less nervous of euro-based investment.

The changeover is going to be squeezed into a short time period around the end of 2001. People in Euroland are going to have to wrestle with the compulsory conversion of their bank accounts and their pay packets, at the same time as having to learn a new set of values in the shops and getting ready to handle new notes and coins. The transitional period is going to be complicated by the period of dual trading in both national currencies and euros, although the original idea of a six month transition has now been shortened. It will be a different length in different countries.

British businesses were alarmed by the original timetable for entry. Retailers did not like the idea of having to price everything in Euros and in pounds during the January sales, when they are especially busy and would have to double price in each currency with the sale price as well as the original price. Many businesses felt the timetable was too tight for preparation, given all the cash handling machines and computer programmes that needed to be changed. The government, meanwhile, has suggested that businesses should be preparing now for possible entry, giving them a longer time than the Continental firms. This is far from helpful to British business, as there is no guarantee that the government will ever hold a referendum, let alone win one, to make the planning and expenditure necessary.

Chapter nine

The cost to business

The task of changing over a complete national currency to a new one is enormous. There are 20,000 automated teller machines handling the existing type of paper currency note in Britain. All of these would need replacing to handle entirely different styles and shapes of note. There are also 500,000 point-of-sale terminals in shops around the country that would also need fundamental overhaul or replacement to handle the new currency. All accounting and cash settlement systems would need adjusting to deal in the redenominated currency and in the period of transition would need to be able to shift from Sterling to the euro and back again using the fixed conversion factor. Around the European Community as a whole there are 12 billion bank notes in circulation with another 8 billion in store. All or most of these need replacing with new ones. The complete coinage would need re-minting into the new shapes and specifications of the Euro-currency.

Only once before in recent history has Britain embarked upon a fundamental change in its coinage. On that occasion, Britain decided to convert to a decimal currency. It was a gargantuan undertaking for retailers and bankers in particular, and it took many months or years for the public to get used to the new denomination of their coinage. In comparison, converting to the euro will be a far larger operation than decimalisation. In order to smooth the process of decimalisation a relatively straightforward system was developed. Firstly, the £1, £5, £10 and higher denomination banknotes continued in circulation with the same designs and same face value. The main unit of account remained £1 which did not alter its value as a result of decimalisation. In consequence accounting systems and settlement systems had the same large unit of account to handle and all banknote handling machinery remained the same.

Even the reminting of the coinage was made easier by continuing to use those coins from the old coinage which could be used under the redenominated system. While it was not possible to use the old one penny because the new penny had a value 2.4 times greater than the one it was replacing it was possible to continue to use the old sixpence, one shilling and two shilling pieces. The two shilling piece translated exactly into 10 pence under the new system and the two shilling or florin coin continued to circulate to double up as a ten-pence coin during a transitional period. The new 10p coins were minted in the same shape and weight as the two shilling piece they were replacing. Similarly, the one shilling coin translated exactly into 5 pence and was handled in an identical way. Certain coins had to be removed from circulation altogether. The 6d was 2½ new pence – it remained in circulation for several years, although no new 2½p coins were minted. The half-penny under the old system was redundant. The 3d piece did not translate into any round number of new pennies and so that was withdrawn. Completely new coins were issued in the denomination of one new pence and two new pence. For a transitional period, a half new pence coin was issued which had a value 20 per cent higher than the old penny it was replacing.

It still remained a large logistical exercise. Enough half, one and two penny pieces had to be made available on D-Day to ensure smooth functioning of the cash system. A massive public education exercise had to be launched for many months beforehand to try and ease the transition and to give people an understanding of the new values of the coins they would be handling. At the time, inflation was quite rapid and there was a strong feeling that decimalisation fuelled it. Moving from one penny worth a 240th of a pound to a new penny worth one 100th of a pound gave retailers of smaller-priced items scope to round up in a way which favoured their profit margins. People buying smaller value items especially food stuffs took some time to adjust to the new sense of values. They had to remember that if they saw something marked in pence they had to multiply that by 2.4 times to give the equivalent in old pennies. It was a great relief to most that the pound unit had not changed so that their sense of values for the higher priced items remained unchanged.

In the case of a small shopkeeper, the costs will be very considerable. For a period of up to six months if Britain joins a single currency all shops in Britain will have to make available facilities to buy goods in both sterling and Euros. In practice this will mean doubling up the number of tills in the shop to handle two separate sets of banknotes and coins. Because the banknotes and coins will all be different from each other and because the conversion rate between the two will be a difficult one (something like 1 euro = 63p), there will be no alternative but to have double the existing number of tills, with shop assistants taking money in the different currencies according to the choice of the customer. It is a legal requirement of the system that for the transitional period customers can settle in either currency.

Each shop will therefore need a larger working cash balance or float each day. It may well be possible to make some estimates of the relative balance of usage of the new and old currency avoiding the need simply to double the balances. However the shop will need something approaching double the cash particularly in the early days before they know the likely pattern of use between the two currencies. The pattern of use is also likely to change over time as you would expect use of the euro to grow as people got more accustomed to it and as more euro coins were pumped into circulation through the banking system.

A storekeeper if he has point-of-sale equipment, will also need to re-program or replace that point of sale equipment to handle debit and credit cards denominated in Euros, settling through the euro system rather than the domestic sterling system. The shopkeeper will need to price everything in both currencies and will doubtless also have to help educate the public. It would be particularly complicated if customers wished to use a mixture of the two currencies to pay for a given item. The shopkeeper may well accommodate their wish, but it would entail complex manoeuvres between the two separate tills and accounting systems that the shop is using in the transitional period.

It is for these reasons that the British retailers have come out strongly against any kind of transitional period at all. However, the authorities believe the transitional period is essential both to acclimatise the public to such a big change in their sense of values and the currency of their use and to smooth the path of issuing such a huge number of banknotes and coins into circulation. The authorities do not believe they could get enough notes and coins into all the right places for a single day of entry of the new system. This is a big difference from the way in which Britain introduced her decimal coinage in the 1970s.

British retailers are also very worried about beginning the process of the new euro on 1 January or 2 January. The Christmas and New Year period is one of the busiest retailing periods of the year. It is complicated by the seasonal holiday closures, the introduction of the January sales stock and the surge of buyers taking advantage of the holiday period to do some bargain hunting and shopping. British retailers would far rather see the introduction of the euro delayed by a month to start on 1 February, after they have handled the Christmas and New Year rush and the January sales. In this, they have common sense on their side.

The small shopkeeper will also have to educate himself in the accounting and taxation consequences of the new currency. On current Commission plans, he would have to present euro accounts before the conversion, and he would need to adjust his own thinking to be able to handle both currencies for a long transitional period. The euro will be in circulation in wholesale markets and for corporate purposes for automated settlement clearing many months before the introduction of the notes and coins for the retail customer.

Businesses in the leisure and street vending industry will have an even bigger task than the typical retailer. Anyone running a business selling hot drinks, Coca-Cola, chocolate bars, peanuts, pharmaceutical items or anything else through vending machines will have to change all of their machinery. For the transitional period, they too will need alternative machines or run the risk of losing business when people wish to buy one of their products but do not have the currency that their machinery happens to use at that juncture. Like the retailers, the owners of vending machines will need to increase the cash floats for a given level of retailing as both the euro and the sterling denominated machines will need to have adequate floats to offer change where that is a facility offered by the company.

In the case of amusement and leisure businesses, all of their machinery will also need changing over to handle the euro and for the transitional period, will need to take both currencies. Alternatively it may be possible at the door of the amusement arcade or at a central point in a pleasure park, to offer cash changing facilities so that the machinery could continue to operate on just one currency but it would be a cumbersome way of proceeding. In due course all of the machinery does have to be converted to the new currency anyway. None of these businesses will gain any benefit from the enormous expense of re-equipping as none of them has Deutschmark or French franc business.

All those businesses taking cash from the public in return for goods or services supplied are worried that there will be problems during the transitional period. Difficulty in obtaining the right quantities of cash would place an additional stress and strain on their businesses. It is retailers, above all, else who have to guarantee the flexibility of the transitional period, offering facilities in both sterling and Euros.

The changes for banks and financial businesses are also enormous. The BAC system of automated clearing to clear credits and debits through the exchange of magnetic data on a three day cycle needs converting to the Euro. So too does the cheque clearing and credit clearing systems handling paper transactions and all of the settlement systems for credit and debit cards. Decisions have to be made about how credit and debit cards are going to operate in the transitional period. Will people need a new credit card or debit card when they switch over their bank account to euro denomination or will the automatic adjustment be made on the existing card? Will banks be prepared to run systems that balance up peoples' euro and sterling bank accounts if they decide to have bank accounts in both currencies in the transitional period? Costs of transactions will be greatly increased during the period of dual denomination within both the financial and the retail systems.

The UK already has a real-time settlement system settling payments between member banks within the UK. A typical daily transaction volume of £120 billion is handled through this computerised settlement. If Britain decides to join the single currency, then the CHAPS clearing system will need linking to the target clearing system between those members of the single currency in the European Community. Our own real-time settlement system influenced the design and structure of the new euro target system.

In the 1990s there was a system for settling ecu transactions around the European Community. The ecu banking association operates this system. At the end of each banking day it makes the necessary transfers between the member state banks on a net basis through accounts at the Bank for International Settlement. This might have been developed into a system for the ecu as a single currency. Now that the community has decided to substitute a different system based on a different currency the ecu banking association has had to decide what to do with its system. It faced the prospect of having a system for ECU settlement with no ECU to settle when it was compulsorily abolished and the euro substituted. The ECU Banking Association as a result have decided to switch their settlement system over to handling the Euro. Instead of settling transactions between member state banks across accounts at the Bank for International Settlement, they plan to settle these accounts through the European system of central banks. They are therefore proposing a rival euro settlement system to the target system being established *de novo* as part of the single currency plans.

There is no objection in principle to having two rival systems of euro settlement. Some will say it will reduce the liquidity in either of the settlement systems, which could make it a little less smooth. Others will say that it might mean extra costs by having two rival infrastructures to achieve the same purpose. There is the offsetting possibility that having competitive settlement systems will keep them both up to the mark and limit the scope for either of them to try to charge a monopoly rent by having a monopoly over settlements in the community.

The new euro target settlement system is not cheaper than the systems it is replacing. A great deal of money has been spent on new computerised systems. Massive sums have been spent on consultancy and planning. All this capital will need remunerating and repaying one way or another. The modest savings to international businesses from no foreign exchange transaction cost will in whole or part be offset by the additional costs needed for cash settlement and credit and paper settlement of transactions using the new automated settlement systems.

Companies share capital will need redenominating in Euros instead of sterling. The Stock Exchange will have to change its listing rules which currently include requirements in sterling. During the transitional period Companies will need to offer dividends in sterling as well as in Euros. It is likely that each listed company will have to notify its shareholders of the changeover, seek their approval to changes in the share capital structure when it is redenominated and then circulate them again over their preferences for receiving dividends in sterling or in Euro. Circulating mass shareholders for a public limited company is an expensive operation. The necessary steps to change share capital and dividend arrangements may well entail several mailings and circulations of shareholders.

Corporate accountants and lawyers are worried that the switch to the euro could also trigger tax liabilities. Under the current Commission proposals when currencies are irrevocably locked for those currencies entering the single currency scheme, the Commission proposes, that companies should have to present balance sheets denominated in Euros and crystallise all the profits or losses on currencies at that point.

British companies have two important worries about this proposal. The first is that so doing could crystallise a tax liability, although the underlying changes in foreign exchange have not yet been realised. It is important that the tax authorities should agree throughout the European Community that the transition from national currencies to the euro should make no difference to the tax liability of the company concerned.

The second worry is that this proposal of the Commission will require companies to change their normal accounting procedures. It is not always good accounting procedure in Britain to crystallise all foreign exchange losses or gains before the underlying contracts have been completed. It is one of many examples of how the Commission would use the existence of the single currency scheme to change British and international accountancy arrangements without necessarily thinking about the business consequences.

No one has yet produced a reliable costing of the amount of investment involved. Preliminary suggestions point to a £4,000 million cost to change the banking system over to parallel running and then the introduction of the Euro. This is likely to prove an underestimate. In the case of retailers an independent European assessment has come up with the figure of £3,500 million to switch over British shops to dual running and then the introduction of the Euro. When account is taken of all the other changes needed in public limited companies and small businesses, the change of all cash handling and accounting systems, it is difficult to see how the final bill could be less than £30,000 million. It is rather like imposing a 12p surcharge on income tax on the country as a whole, as little of this investment will be remunerated. As one of the rules of the introduction is that prices should not go up as a result of the introduction of the new currency, the theorists of the scheme are proposing a £30,000 million tax on British business with no means of direct benefit.

In practice, of course, it is likely that prices would go upwards as a result of the transitional period. When companies come to review their pricing practices in the new currency they are likely to round up and claim that the product is a new variant justifying a different price. Proponents of the single currency scheme claim that the reward will come to business in the form of lower interest rates and in the form of saved foreign exchange commissions. As we have seen, most businesses will have no savings on foreign exchange at all because they do not deal in foreign exchange at the moment. Those that do may well face increases in money transmission costs in whole or part off-setting the Foreign Currency Commission Savings. We have also seen that lower interest rates are unlikely. The long-term real rate of interest has been higher in France and in Germany than in Britain in the period 1980 to 1995, and it is difficult to see why this should change as a result of joining the euro block.

A £30,000 million investment would normally require £7,500 million a year of additional revenues to justify it. This would mean a 0.9 per cent increase in prices or raising our inflation rate by around 40 per cent. Proponents of the scheme have to explain why they think this would not happen. They should go back and look at what happened during the period of decimalisation when a much simpler and more modest change none the less triggered rounding up price rises.

Ten costly problems with the changeover

1 Banks need to change all their tills and cash handling twice: once to introduce the euro as a second currency, then to remove the pound when the transition ends.

2 Businesses collecting money from car park machines or turn-stiles need to offer two coin and note set slots for the transitional period, then will have to spend money on blanking out the pound and pence slots.

3 Shoppers will be weighed down with coins in two different currencies. They will need to be able to pay for the whole transaction in one of the two currencies.

4 Shops will need two sets of tills for the transition, one to handle pounds and one to handle euros.

5 The January sales will need four prices on the tickets:normal and sale price in both pounds and euros.

6 People will have no sense of values in Euros at first. It will be like shopping in a foreign currency.

7 For a UK business trading only in the UK, it will be all cost and no benefit – and that's most UK businesses.

8 For an international trading business, the cost will outweigh the benefit.

9 It is likely to cost British business more than £30 billion in total. What return could they possible earn on this, when most will see no cost savings at all?

10 There will be little or no saving on bank charges. There will still be a charge to settle accounts and pay cheques across frontiers, even if they are in the same currency. So far, money transmission costs have gone up with the Euro.

Chapter ten

Renegotiation – the best course

Britain needs to renegotiate its deal in the European Community as a whole. The Conservative opposition in Parliament is pledged to renegotiate several aspects of our relationships with the European Community. The government is unable to plunge into all the centralising policies favoured by the Commission and some of our partners. We need a better deal for our fishermen. We would like more control over the money we spend on overseas aid and development, as the EC spends it so badly on our behalf. We need fundamental revisions to the common agricultural policy, a reduction in the EU budget, less regulation and a stronger voice for free trade. The UK, whoever is in government, cannot go along with plans for Brussels to have more power over taxation, frontiers, foreign policy, defence or the economy.

Many in the country feel that, having joined the Common Market the European Community has moved too far away from this original intention. Instead of more trade, it is giving us more government. Instead of furthering our prosperity, many of the rules, regulations and economic policies are actively impeding economic progress. The cry is going up around the country that

201

the government should negotiate to get us back to something closer to the Common Market we joined, further away from the European Union or European country that France and Germany are trying to create.

The single currency is crucial to any future re-negotiation of our relationships with the partner economies of western Europe. The single currency, as we have seen, is the most important step on the federal road that any participating country could take. It is the crucial step to move from a national economic policy to a European economic policy. It represents a substantial transfer of wealth and power from the national institutions to the European institutions. The question is 'could Britain re-negotiate a better deal in Europe without threatening withdrawal or being forced into withdrawal'?

There are many who say that the progress of the European Union towards a country called Europe is inevitable. They believe that Britain has no influence over these events, unless Britain goes along with them. They see no future for Britain outside the European Community and no future for Britain as the difficult partner within. Yet any analysis of the position shows that if Britain wished to she could have important, if not decisive, influence over the future direction of European Community policy.

The negotiations for the Amsterdam and Nice Treaties showed a timid Britain throwing away its power and its opportunity. We could have demanded more in both those sets of negotiations before surrendering our veto, before giving the others permission to go ahead with the schemes they favour. At Nice, the UK was particularly craven. We did not table our vision of what was wanted. We confined ourselves to damage limitation, seeking to remove only the more extreme tax and immigration powers that the EU sought and then claiming victory. Worse still, by granting permission to the others to go ahead without us under a procedure allowing "enhanced co-operation" we limited our scope to use the veto in future to get something back that we want. Even so, there will remain opportunities in the future when our partners will need our agreement to something they want to do. Next time we must use the power this brings to get something we want in return.

Wielding the veto gives Britain substantial power. It is quite clear that Britain's view of a Europe of nations is not compatible with a common foreign and defence policy, nor with more qualified majority voting nor with strengthened powers for the Commission, the Parliament and the Council of Ministers. To have a proper Europe of nations, we need a transfer of powers away from the European institutions back to member states governments and more particularly back to companies, individuals and families out of the hands of government altogether. We should, therefore, table our own agenda of genuine decentralisation, deregulation, and the shedding of government power. We should demand this as our price for going along with any of the radical schemes that France and Germany favour for more integration between themselves. They want to use Community money and Community institutions for their plans.

Some say it is not feasible for Britain to carry on opting out of different parts of the Community's procedures. History tells us otherwise. Britain negotiated an opt-out from the Social Chapter, keeping more power to legislate over social and employment matters at home rather than exporting it to Brussels. A subsequent British government foolishly gave this opt-out away for nothing in return. We have also negotiated the right not to join the single currency, the most fundamental opt-out of them all. Britain has protected her right to keep her own borders and has said she will not co-operate with the Schengen scheme of common frontiers. Britain still has a veto over many matters of taxation, foreign policy and defence policy.

It is quite possible to construct a Community based upon flexible architecture. Those who wish the Community to take on a foreign and defence policy role have not yet suggested that a country such as Ireland in order to remain a member of the Community will have to surrender her position of neutrality. Nor should they insist on this. If Ireland wishes to remain as a neutral country she should be able to do so while still continuing to be a good member of the Community in every other respect. Similarly, if Britain wishes to keep her own economic policy separate from that of her partners but remain a member of the single market why should she not do so? We never pledged nor promised in 1972 when we first joined the Community that we would definitely abolish the pound and join a single currency scheme at a later date. There would be no bad faith in Britain wishing to preserve her right to self-government in this important area.

The precedent of opt-out shows that it can be done. The criticism then turns to the proposition that we would not be able to negotiate further opt-outs because our partners are sick and tired of Britain following a different course. Again, history does not bear out this criticism. Given that they need our vote to secure the radical changes they wish, of course it would be possible to negotiate an opt out. If France and Germany is faced with the proposition that they cannot go ahead with their own defence and foreign policy merger unless Britain is given an opt-out from it then I am sure they will choose the lesser of two evils from their point of view and settle on the merger while giving Britain an opt out.

Some suggest that it is not a moral position of Britain to delay progress towards a European state in this way. I would argue the opposite; that it is not fair that France and Germany constantly wish to use our common Community institutions for a purpose to which we never gave our consent. Nobody told us honestly when we joined the Community in the first place that we would be expected to pay the bills and to offer our vote in support of the creation of a massive new Government for Europe as a whole. Now that this is coming to pass it is not unreasonable for Britain to say that we do not wish to be part of those developments and we have no wish to pay the bills.

If France and Germany wish to merge their economies, their foreign policy, their defence policy that ultimately is a matter for them and their Governments. It becomes a matter for us if they wish to use our common institutions and have access to British tax payers money in order to do so; then Britain has every right to say "No".

Some say that using the veto to this considerable extent is

tantamount to withdrawing from the European Community altogether. It is difficult to understand this argument. If somebody joins a cricket club and then discovers that some of the other members wish to change the rules to turn it into a rugby club as well it would not be unreasonable for the person who had joined the cricket club believing it to be just a cricket club to oppose the change of rules to make it a rugby club in addition. He could rightly say that he wished his subscription only to go to the support of cricket and did not wish to have to bear a bigger subscription in order to cover the cost of rugby fixtures during the winter. Under the normal rules of most clubs this person could not be expelled because he did not recommend a change in the rules and aims and purposes of the club that he had joined in good faith. Indeed, most people would think that the conduct of the members of the club who wished to make it a rugby club as well was less reasonable than the conduct of the member who wished to keep it as it was. The obvious answer would be for those wanting rugby would be to set up a separate rugby club. This is the position in which Britain finds herself vis a vis the European Community.

The European Community is a legal construct based on treaty and interpretation of the treaty through the European Court. There is no clause or power in the treaty to expel a member of the Community. Whatever Britain did, the Community would be faced with the proposition that legally it could not remove us. There is certainly no power in treaty or in natural law or natural justice that would enable the Community members to expel Britain because she had vetoed a number of proposals they supported. Nor would it be in the interests of Germany and France to try and get us out of the Community. Although they find it vexatious that we hold up a number of the changes they wish to see, they do find our £10,000 million a year contribution extremely useful and they do enjoy trading with us as they sell us far more than we sell them. It is difficult to believe that Germany would reach the point where she said to us 'Please do not buy our BMW's any more' or France would reach the point where she said 'Please take the money away which you are currently giving to the poorer regions of France'. Both France and Germany know that it is in their trading and commercial interest to do business with Britain and both know that Britain is a fully paid up and legal member of the European Community.

What should Britain seek in the renegotiations? Britain should set out a shopping list of its requirements both for a more prosperous and successful Community as a whole and for a happier relationship for Britain with it.

Britain's agenda for Europe should be an agenda to promote business and jobs. European Government is getting in the way of prosperity. It is the high interest and exchange rates required by the Maastricht treaty that have done so much damage to Continental levels of employment. It is the laws and regulations from Brussels that are destroying the capacity of small business to expand and grow, to create the jobs that people need. Britain should set out an agenda based on flexible exchange rates, the end of the Exchange Rate Mechanism, fewer rules and regulations and markets more open to business success.

It is no accident that British levels of unemployment are now one third lower than the Community average. Nor is it an accident which gives to Asia and America lower levels of unemployment than Britain. We must learn from their successes. Britain should propose deregulation of big industries like financial services, telecommunications and media where many of the future jobs will lie. Britain should set out a list of two or three hundred directives that are no longer needed or impede business success. The Community is in danger of stifling technical innovation. It does not need 40 different directives specifying how you make different parts for a car in order to have a successful motor industry in Western Europe. Specifying too many things in legislation can make it illegal to improve or change products and components. Nor does it make sense to have such high levels of social protection for workers that companies are unable to afford enough employees so that many millions of people stay on the dole.

Britain should insist that the principal aim of European policy should be the promotion of employment and prosperity. More than 18 million people are out of work in the European Community. That is more than the entire populations of Luxembourg, Ireland, Finland, Portugal and Greece put together. It is a sad testimony to political failure on a grand scale. The European Community now regularly meets and shakes its head about the problem and proposes small packages of measures based on the principle that you buy jobs by spending more public money. There is a double irony in this policy. Firstly, increasing Community spending means that more important programmes have to be cut in domestic budgets in order to meet the Maastricht convergence criteria. Secondly, it fails to understand that jobs come from a dynamic private enterprise sector and not from recycling money through the public sector.

The UK should explain how a deregulated telecoms and multi-media industry could be the centrepiece for massive economic growth and expansion in the next century. America has been much more successful than Western Europe at telecommunications and multi-media based upon the policy of deregulation, competition and choice. By backing state monopolies, protective legislation and political intervention Europe has delivered less at much greater cost. CNN dominates world news gathering. Hollywood dominates the world film industry. Ma Bell and her offshoots dominate the world telecommunications links. Only Britain with a deregulated telecoms industry and the first signs of a deregulated media industry is making some impact.

Britain should expect a far better deal for her fishermen. I was shocked when I visited Lowestoft to learn that a once great fishing port had fallen on extremely hard times. When we joined the European Community, 100 large British trawlers operated out of Lowestoft and plied a successful trade. Today there are just 10 left. There has been a 90 per cent reduction in the Lowestoft trawler fleet. Under the current proposals from the EU Commissioner another four of those ten vessels would have to disappear leaving just 6 per cent of the fishing fleet the European Community inherited in 1972. On the day I visited, a normal working day, just one vessel came back to port with a catch. It took fifteen minutes to sell the fish in the fish market and that was the end of the day's work for all involved. When I asked where the other 9 vessels were I was told they could not fish that day because they did not have sufficient quota to entitle them to do so. The British Isles are surrounded by fertile seas with many shoals of good fish. They have been over-fished in no small measure by Spanish and Dutch vessels. Today many British vessels have to stay moored by the quayside and the fishermen watch as the Spanish and Dutch vessels come in and take our fish. If the Community will not give us a major increase in our quota at the expense of the Spanish and Dutch interlopers then Britain should reassert her 200-mile territorial limit and reclaim the fish for herself. We could then reduce the total quota for fishing while massively increasing the quota that goes to the British fleet. Both conservation and the British industry would be well served by such a policy. What is stopping us?

Some say it would not be legal for Britain to re-assert her 200-mile limits. All the legislation is in place as the 200-mile limit currently operates for other resources of the deep. Aggregates dredged from the sea bed, oil, gas and similar natural assets are governed by a 200-mile or a median point exclusion zone. All we would need to do is add fish into the relevant statute and regulations. Indeed, Mrs Bonino when Fisheries Commissioner said that it lies in our own hands to settle the fishing industry. I presume this is what she had in mind.

However, threatening to do this would have such a big impact upon the Dutch and Spanish industries that I am sure the European Community would soon want to talk about a better deal for Britain. We might well be able to negotiate a satisfactory increase in our quotas and a reduction in Spanish and Dutch quotas if we proposed as an alternative the reintroduction of our own territorial limits.

Some say that it would not be realistic to patrol the new territorial waters. Yet this is what we used to do before the common fisheries policy was introduced and that is exactly what countries like Canada do against the interlopers from Spain. In the last Canadian/Spanish fish war the British public were firmly on the side of the Canadians and many Canadian flags were seen flying in the ports on the harbours of Britain to show solidarity for what the Canadians were doing. It could be done if we have a will to do it.

The European Court: servant or master?

The biggest problem we need to tackle is the power of the European Court of Justice. It is the European Court of Justice that is trying to undermine our opt out from the social chapter. Their decision on the 48-hour working week directive has decided that this particular piece of European legislation is governed by health and safety which we do have to accept and not by the Social Chapter which we do not. It is becoming a dangerous back door to force through in Britain a number of social and employment measures which the government in good faith felt it had excluded Britain from accepting. It is the European Court of Justice which is the most federal of all the institutions. The Court's judges believe it is their role in life to push ever onward in a federal direction. They interpret the general preambles of the treaty in a generous way. They accept that the whole purpose of Community development is to create a country called Europe with an ever bigger government from Brussels and Frankfurt.

Some say there is nothing we can do about the growing powers of the Court. They say that we signed away our Parliamentary supremacy when we joined the Community in 1972. They say that it is a ratchet, it will continue to turn against us and we must accept growing powers for the Community as adjudicated by the European Court. This is fatalism of the worst kind. What an Act of Parliament can grant it can take back. Our constitution is based upon two important propositions. The first is that an Act of Parliament is always sovereign. The second is that a Parliament cannot bind its successors. Only an Act of Parliament can overturn an Act of Parliament. The whole purpose of democratic general elections is to decide which team of politicians the public would like to see legislating or not legislating on their behalf. If a new team is elected it has the perfect right subject to the manifesto and to public opinion to change any Act of Parliament it inherits in the interests of the nation as it sees them.

This system has been gravely disrupted by the intrusion of the European Court of Justice. In practice, a Parliament has now bound its successors in an ever more restrictive way. The 1972 European Communities Act gives the European Court of Justice the power it needs to adjudicate cases affecting Britain. The European Court has moved from just adjudicating cases to interpreting and making law. The Court has decided it can overturn Acts of Parliament and Parliament so far has accepted this judgement. Unless Parliament challenges this principle soon then Parliamentary democracy as we know it has effectively been abolished. There will be an ever growing range of issues which will not be settled by elected politicians in a free Parliament but which have or will be decided by a group of unelected Judges in a far away Court. Already Government Ministers thinking of proposing legislation to the House of Commons have to ask first of all whether their legislation would be legal under European Law. As European Law expands it will become evermore important to know who makes European Law and how it is made and ever less important to win votes in the House of Commons. So what can be done to remedy this problem?

I would suggest a simple one clause Act of Parliament. This Act of Parliament would say that the European Court of Justice cannot overturn an Act of Parliament unless Parliament consents. The European Court of Justice should be able to advise, warn or urge that Britain amends its Acts of Parliament to bring them into line with the European Court's view of our treaty obligations. But if we wish to remain living in a Parliamentary democracy ultimately Parliament must decide what our treaty obligations comprise and how we wish to honour them. If Parliament decides that a Government in good faith had opted us out of certain types of European legislation and if Parliament votes to reaffirm that, that should be the end of the matter. We should not have to accept laws because the European Court has said it disagrees with our view of the treaty we signed in good faith.

Some say that this would not work. They say that if we pass such as Act of Parliament the British Courts might not obey it. The British Courts might say that they believe that the European Court of Justice was supreme and that they would refuse to co-operate in implementing a law passed by Parliament which did not have the consent or agreement of the European Court of Justice as well. Our constitutional history used to be littered with disputes of this nature between the King, Parliament and Courts in the 16th and 17th Centuries. They were resolved then in favour of Parliamentary supremacy. So should these disputes be resolved today if such disputes still arise. If British Judges in a British Court refuse to uphold the will of Parliament, the British Supreme Court, then Parliament would have to change the British Courts until they did come in line with the democratic will of the majority as expressed in Parliament.

Some argue that if we took this view it would be tantamount to leaving the European Community. Again I disagree. Germany has done something similar already. In an important judgement of the German Constitutional Court, that Court has said that if a European Court ruling is in disagreement with the German Constitution then ultimately the German Constitution and the German Parliament will prevail. If that is good enough for Germany, why can't something similar be good enough for Britain? There is no power to expel a member of the Community. To pass an Act of Parliament along the lines described would only bring us back to the position many people thought we were in when we joined the European Community in the first place.

Others say that the weakness in doing this is to undermine the credibility of the European Court itself. They say that the European Court is more likely to be in our favour than against. They say that we need a strong European Court to ensure the fair and firm enforcement of common rules across the Community. What would happen, they say, to a British business needing access to the French market protected by European rules if the European Court was not there to enforce it against French jurisdiction?

Under the system where an Act of Parliament is sovereign it has to be assumed that a British democratic Parliament would act in good faith. A British Parliament would not try to overturn rules and regulations which the British Government had agreed to within the Community. Nor would it try to enforce a view clearly against that set out in the treaty. All the British Parliament would be trying to do is to ensure that the treaty we thought we had signed is the treaty that actually operates in Britain. While it is true that some British litigants do win cases in the European Court of Justice, it is also true to say that there have been a number of notable failures. The failure of the Community to take action against continental countries offering huge subsidies to their businesses to compete unfairly against British ones is worrying. The failure of the Court to deal with all of the restrictions to trade in a country like France is also flagrant. The use of the Court in opening up the continental market to Britain has been distinctly limited.

We should propose in the inter-Governmental conference the new settlement for the Court to try and avoid the need for unilateral action. We should try to get all countries to agree that their ultimate constitutional right must be to put through their own interpretation of the treaty. If you believe in a Europe of Nations that ultimately must be the position. There could be some new cases where this meant that a common rule was not properly enforced in a continental country against Britain's interests. It would also mean, however, that Britain could solve a number of its own big problems with the Community without any other legal trouble. We would gain much more than we lost.

Restoring the sovereignty of an Act of Parliament would enable us to solve the fishing problem. A short one clause bill would then extend the 200 mile limit and median zone to cover fish and again it could not be subject to interference from the European Community.

Under fear of us passing such an Act of Parliament it is very likely the European Community would offer a compromise limiting the power of the European Court of Justice to intervene in areas which we believe to be beyond its competence under the treaty we signed. I am sure they would immediately be forth-coming with proper protection on social and employment matters to back up the protection we thought we had secured at Maastricht. They might well throw in proper protection over borders and frontiers which is the next area they are likely to move in on and they might well offer us a better deal on beef and fish.

All of this shows that constructive negotiating progress could be made if we combined carrot and stick. The carrot must be two fold. We must always consider compromise when they start to meet our needs and we should offer them the prospect of us agreeing to allow further federal progress for them if they look after our interests separately. The stick must be to have in mind a series of measures which could solve the problem by direct and unilateral action if the community fails to give us what we need.

Many on the continent think the question for Britain is a timing one, not a difference of opinion over the fundamental direction. So far they have been proved right. The UK was unable to join the EEC when it began, but joined later. We were unwilling to join the Social Chapter when it commenced, but have done so since. Surely, say our partners, it will be the same with the currency? A few more months or a few more years, and slow old Britain will catch up. Discussion is of two speed Europe, not of two track Europe.

Many of us want it to be different this time round. We want a variegated Europe of different clubs and different groupings. We do not want to join a monetary union, nor a defence union. We want to keep the pound and continue with NATO. There is big tussle underway over who will be proved right. All the time the British people remain so adamant that an integrated Europe is not for them, the UK will stay out of the Euro. Although there are many other centralising tendencies which are disliked or damaging, the euro has become the centre of the debate, the litmus test of how committed we are, because it is the only central policy of the EU where we will be given a separate vote, where our views matter.

Many people in the UK see the debate in terms of whether we join Europe or not. They think all the time we are outside the currency we are somehow outside the whole thing. Many are unaware of just how tied up in it all we are already. If you explain it to them they express surprise and sometimes horror that so much power has slipped across the Channel with no-one debating it or asking for popular consent. All too many British people see Europe as over there – they do not regard themselves as European or think Britain is part of Europe. Even some of the most avid protagonists of European integration will ask revealing questions of me such as "Do you ever go to Europe?"

It is time that debate was joined in the UK. We cannot go on living a lie on both sides of the Channel. If the government wants us to sign up to the full economic, monetary and political union it should say so, argue the case, and try to win consent in a referendum. If they are forced to admit that's not what a majority of us want, they should set out to our partners how far we can go, and what we need to bring back, so that people once again feel they live in a self governing UK democracy.

I find more and more British people dismayed to learn how much power has gone, while political leaders on the continent want to model Europe on the lines of the German federation, where England will be to the EU as Bavaria is to Germany. Such a vision is incompatible with vibrant national Parliamentary democracy. When the German Foreign Minister and the German Ambassador recently told me that they understood we wished to keep our Parliament and we would be allowed to do so I did not find it reassuring. For their vision is of a Europe which settles foreign policy, economic policy, immigration policy, environmental policy and trade policy. It would not leave much for all the MPs to discuss. There's no point taking the nut out of the shell, and then presenting the shell as a delicacy to eat. We need to debate where power should lie, where we want it to lie, where it is going to lie. If we said Yes to the currency a great deal of power would have gone from our island democracy to their continental bureaucracy. If we say No, we have a chance of rescuing the rest of our liberty. Our freedom was hard fought, hard won, hard defended. I do not believe most British people wish to give it away in such a stealthy fashion. That's why it's better to say No.

Ten things we need to renegotiate

1 We need to repatriate fishing policy, to prevent even more damage to our fishing industry from the Common Fisheries Policy.

2 We need to reform the Common Agricultural Policy radically to make it more useful to consumers and British farmers.

3 We need to curb the waste and fraud in the EU overseas aid budget, and have more control over our spending in this area.

4 We need to de-regulate the Single market, removing many of the expensive and unnecessary rules.

5 We need to undo those parts of the Amsterdam and Nice Treaties which make it more difficult for us to have an independent foreign policy.

6 We need to limit the power of the European Court, so it cannot overturn Acts of Parliament.

7 We need to restore our right to make our own social and employment rules.

8　We need to agree with our partners that we can join NAFTA as well as the EU single market.

9　We need a fairer deal on how much we contribute to the EU, as we wish to limit its power and bureaucracy.

10　We need to ensure that the EU army is under NATO control.

How Europe could become more prosperous without a United States of Europe

Ten differences between the UK and Euroland

1 The UK has strong links with the English speaking world.
2 The UK is more a service oriented economy: the main Euroland ones are more manufacturing based.
3 The UK is an oil producer, the others are oil consumers.
4 The UK has less unemployment than the main countries of Euroland.
5 The UK has enjoyed lower taxes than Euroland.
6 The UK economy is more open to the world and more dependent on non EU trade than the other EU countries.
7 The UK takes an Anglo-Saxon attitude to competition and company control, believing in the challenge of takeovers. Euroland favours bank and family control and no contested takeovers.
8 The UK has had less regulation than Euroland.
9 UK attitudes are more entrepreneurial, disliking too much government intervention and involvement in business.

10 The UK is a longer established democracy than many on the
continent, where people expect taxes and laws to be openly
debated and criticised in Parliament first.

The French and German Governments are totally committed to
economic, monetary and political union. At Nice, negotiating yet
another treaty to carry forward their ideal, there were some
tensions and disagreements between the big two, but the process
rolls on. Two years ago there were still considerable doubts and
uncertainties about monetary union. That is now a done deal.
The question now is how far and how fast they go in developing
their common foreign policy, European army, common borders
and the other items to complete the construction of a United
States of Europe.

London needs to remain offshore from the euro area whether
Britain has joined it or not. The City of London relies upon
running big dollar and yen and other markets and relies upon
free movements of capital around the world. It would not
flourish under Frankfurt style banking controls. Euroenthusiasts
believe that we have little freedom of monetary policy at the
moment. This is based on the unwarranted assumption that we
wish to keep the pound stable against the Deutschmark and that
this would determine our monetary policy. As I have shown,
when we did this we did lose our freedom for manoeuvre and we
ripped out the stabilisers that would otherwise have cushioned
the UK economy. Now that we are no longer trying to keep the
pound in line with a particular level of the Deutschmark, we have
considerable freedom of monetary policy. If the European

Central Bank increases or reduces its interest rates tomorrow there is no need for Britain to follow suit. We would have to follow suit if we were worried about the consequences of the euro move for the exchange rate.

Some say the single market needs a single money. This argument is a slippery slope. If we concede it, the next argument will be that a single market needs a single tax policy, otherwise it is unfair. There is no reason why anyone should single out currency fluctuations amongst all the differences and divergences there are between the different European economies. Soon we will hear the argument that you need to harmonise the labour laws and make sure that social and pension costs are similar around the community.

The theory of international trade is based upon the theory that different countries and companies have different advantages which they should reinforce. International trade requires specialisation and it requires an admission on the part of the trading partners that one country is favoured at one thing and another at another. There is no reason why other community countries should have a share of our oil because nature happens to have blessed us with oil any more than there would be any justice in saying that because the Mediterranean countries have a better climate enabling them to grow citrus fruits and olives, we ought to have a share of their citrus and olive crop. We should welcome the fact that different levels of educational achievement, different climates, different skills in the work force, different levels of costs and different exchange rates add to the variety of the international market place.

Euroenthusiaists admit that it will require a huge popular education campaign if the euro is to be successfully introduced and if a referendum is to be won. Polls show that fewer than one quarter of the British people currently support the single currency. The *Sun*'s poll showed that only 1 in 20 supported the single currency; the more general opinion polls suggest that support for it is often well below one fifth of the electorate. People are naturally suspicious of the single currency. They realise that it is the transfer of more that coinage. Of course it represents a huge transfer of sovereignty from Britain to the continent.

There is a positive case to be made out for keeping the pound. The question of what is an optimum area for a currency union is a difficult one. Twenty years ago Southern Ireland decided that the Sterling currency union was too large and separated their own currency from the rest of us. In the late 1980's Scottish nationalists felt they would like to do something similar for Scottish economy. They remained in a small minority, with most Scottish people feeling that a currency and political union with England was still in their best interest. These are matters of national identity. If we ever reached the point where a strong majority of the Scottish people felt they were more Scottish than British and wished to be self governing then of course they would have to leave not only the UK but also the UK single currency scheme.

The example of the United States of America has held out as one which shows that large currency unions can be very successful. It is true that the United States of America has achieved dramatic growth and prosperity in the twentieth century as a currency union. It is also true that the United States of America achieved even more phenomenal economic development in the 19th century when it was not a currency union. The creation of the dollar as the American single currency was an important part of the expression of nationhood of the American peoples. It has caused considerable economic difficulties in some parts of the American union. These have had to be offset as best they can by subsidies and transfer payments.

Britain has a lot to be proud of in the last twenty years. She has achieved a higher rate of growth than her European partners. She has tackled many of the difficulties of burgeoning public sector budgets and welfare spending before her continental partners have managed to do so. By deregulation and free enterprise policies she has created considerable strength for herself in new areas like multi-media, telecommunications, business services, financial services, legal services and pharmaceuticals. All of these industries sell around the world. They are particularly strong in selling in English speaking territories. While Britain exports capital around the world she is particularly keen on exporting capital to the large American market where common a language and culture makes investment and business activity easier.

Britain should keep the pound and think globally. The future lies in the global market using the English language and mobilising large amounts of talent and capital through the City of London and through companies large and small founded in or operating from a UK base.

It is Britain that must have the task of warning Europe before it is too late that single currencies without political unions cannot work, that we need a common market but not a common Government, and that the schemes of over Government devised for Brussels and Frankfurt will do more damage to the competitiveness of Western Europe.

As different aspects of the single currency scheme are revealed to the British people, so they become more worried by it. There was a sense of shock when the public first recognised that our gold and convertible currency reserves would be transferred to Frankfurt and would no longer be used on our behalf at our request. There was another sense of in justice, when it emerged that one way or another the unfunded pension liabilities in France and Germany would come back to haunt us if we had joined a currency union with them. In 1996 people saw the impact of common policies on our fishing industry and our beef industry all too vividly. They began to say to themselves could they really trust economic and monetary policy to the same type of people and institutions that were reeking such havoc in our agricultural and marine industries.

Keep the pound and keep your country. The abolition of the pound is not a mere technical matter for bankers. It goes to the heart of Parliamentary democracy. Once a country has joined a single currency controlled by an independent central bank in a far away city there is no point in discussing many of the important matters of economic policy in General Elections or in Parliamentary Debate. There would be nothing that British politicians could do if your business was unable to obtain credit, if your house price was plummeting because interest rates were too high, if you were unable to export to America or Japan because the level of the euro had soared against those currencies or if taxes went up to pay for the resulting mess in the currency union. The single currency is a massive step on the road to the creation of a country called Europe. It is being created by technocrats. Its power will be operated behind closed doors without proper democratic debate. The record of the technocrats so far is lamentable. Their Exchange Rate Mechanism blew up in their hands. It did untold damage to millions of families, depressing their house prices, destroying many jobs and throwing many businesses into bankruptcy. Now the technicians tell us that they should be trusted with ultimate power in a bank in Frankfurt. They tell us that the Exchange Rate Mechanism did not work, not because it was flawed in concept but because their powers did not go far enough in controlling and directing our lives.

Britain must say no before it is too late. Britain must use her vote and her voice to veto this crazy scheme. Britain must say that the peoples of Western Europe are worth more than a single currency and that their livelihoods and futures are at risk. Britain must say that consent is needed to Government. Countries of Western Europe are finding it difficult enough to keep consent, with Southern and Northern Italians unsure about a Government from Rome, with North and South Belgium unsure about a Government from Brussels, with Basques unsure about Government from Madrid or Paris and Scottish Nationalists unhappy with Government from London. It will not create a happier Europe if they knew more remote central Government authority is imposed on top from Brussels. Far from assuaging regional and local feelings, it will serve to inflame them further.

The concept of European Union and integration died with the collapse of the Holy Roman Empire. It died on the fields of Flanders and in the streets of Berlin in 1945. It should not be revived by peaceful means. The Western European peoples are better off living in peace one with another, organising their Governments at a more local level than Brussels. To force union upon them against their will or against the background of their marked reluctance to accept it can but create more misery and difficulty for the peoples of Western Europe.

The biggest lie put around by those who favour the euro in Britain is that this has nothing to do with the creation of a super-state. Many of them assure us they are as opposed as I am to such a creature. The Prime Minister, Mr Blair, has gone so far as to say he wants the EU to be a superpower but not a superstate. He has not yet managed to explain how you can have the one without the other.

This book has shown that the EU is systematically expanding the power of the bureaucracy in Brussels, of the Courts in Strasbourg, and taking steps to create all the institutions of a superstate. It is a sign of how far they have come that the euro is now taken for granted, and they are already on to building the next steps of their union, before the UK and Denmark have decided whether to join, and before the Euroland countries have completed the transition and fully adopted the new currency.

For the UK the decision to adopt the euro would be a funda-mental one. It would mark the end of hundreds of years of history as an independent and increasingly democratic country.

It would mean a revolution in the way we are governed, switching substantial power from our democracy to their bureaucracy. Britain is an unwilling partner in the superstate venture. Even a Euroenthusiast government like the present one has had to veto the more extreme proposals for common taxation and more Brussels centralisation. Even this government is unsure of whether it can hold a referendum on the Euro. Britain needs to clear the air and have a proper debate. You should only vote Yes to the euro you want to become a citizen of a United States of Europe. If you prefer your British identity and democracy, you must vote No. The sooner we get the issue out of the way the better. We need to negotiate a better relationship with our EU partners, which lets us trade with them and do things together when it makes sense, but does not give away our right to self government. The sooner we do so, the better it will be for us and for them. The Commission and leading continental governments are tired of Britain dragging her heels. Britain is tired of being pilloried and forced into decisions she does not like. Let's have a vote, and let's Just Say No.

Ten things wrong with a superstate

1 People feel loyalty to the UK, not to the EU.
2 British people do not want to send their sons and daughters into battle to fight for the EU.
3 UK voters do not trust continental governments and bureaucracies: they invent the rules, we impose them.
4 UK voters do not think the amounts of money put in and

taken out by the different countries are fair. We make too large a net contribution.

5 We do not feel the same willingness to pay money to those in need in Sicily or Greece as those in Bradford or Liverpool.

6 It is very difficult running a single country that has so many different languages and outlooks.

7 There are great cultural, religious and political differences that would be difficult to bridge in one country.

8 There are substantial transport difficulties making a sense of belonging difficult in a region stretching from Sweden to Portugal, from Greece to Ireland.

9 There is a long tradition of nationalism in Europe.

10 No-one has given their consent in Britain to a superstate, and no-one in government has explained the plan honestly to the electorate.